Out & Allied

Volume 2

An Anthology of Performance Pieces by LGBTQ Youth & Allies

Edited by Cathy Plourde, Meghan Brodie, Elise Orme,
Jack Whelan and Zabet NeuCollins

addverb Publications

D0062466

addverb Publications
A division of addverb Productions, a program of the Westbrook College of
    Health Professions, University of New England
716 Stevens Avenue
Portland, Maine 04103
info@addverbproductions.org
www.addverbproductions.org

The work in this book is made to be performed and may be reformatted for
performance while staying true to the intentions of the authors. You are free
to do so without royalty. If you would care to send a donation to an LGBTQ
agency of some sort or even back to addverb, please also notify us, as we'd
love to know.

ISBN-13: 978-0991352807 (addverb Publications)
ISBN-10: 0991352807
LCCN: 2014900602

The following are used with kind permission of:
- LGBTQ Glossary, GLSEN
- Dreams of Hope performance pieces, Dreams of Hope
- Being LGBTQ in the 21st Century, Liberty Hill Foundation
- Additional Advocacy, Human Rights Campaign
- Where the Wild Things Are: Enhancing Resilience in LGBTQ Youth, Jeff Levy
- "My Mind Was Changed" Toolkit, Auburn Media, Fenton and Goodwin Simon Strategic Research

Photo Credit : Johnny Speckman (back cover)

Cover Design by Sidd Trip and Lauren Johnson, Proactive Resources

*This book is dedicated Betsy Parsons
who has provided a lifeline for youth, families,
and teachers who need it,
and has also found a way to inspire others
to join her in doing the same.*

TABLE OF CONTENTS

PERFORMANCE PIECES

Resources

Acknowledgements and Thank Yous

To all of the LGBTQ advocates and leaders upon whose shoulders this work stands.

To the Team from Out & Allied Vol. 1 for setting the bar so high.

To all of the Faith-based communities who have upheld and applied their faith's values — walked their talk, maintain judgment-free communities and continue to open their hearts and minds.

To the Mukti Fund, PW Sprague Memorial Foundation for their generous funding. To Lauren Johnson and Sidd Tripp of Proactive Resources for cover design extraordinare.

To the Pride Youth Theatre Alliance — the adults and youth who have made queer and allied youth theatre a happening event in the US, many of whom have work represented in this volume and whose work will continue inspire more creative works and life shaping conversations.

To those whose works are either represented here or inspired our direction: Liberty Hill for use of infographics; Human Rights Campaign for re-printing of their resources; Ted Fickes, Brightplus3 blog; Jeff Levey at Live Oak; JQY; Auburn Media, Fenton and Goodwin Simon Strategic Research for compiling the "My Mind Was Changed Toolkit."

To the Faith-Based leaders and the Youth Leaders who make this happen on the ground: Rev. Marvin Ellison, Lucky Hollander, and the Religious Coalition Against Discrimination; Rev. William Gregory; Rabbi Carolyn Braun.

To Mark Fairman, Maya Brown, Treva deMaynadier and all from the S.T.A.N.D, Waterville Inclusive Community Project, and the newly minted Out & Allied Youth Theatre; Brianna Suslovic

To those who have given us a roof — the Westbrook College of Health Professions at the University of New England; Timmi, Rory, and Amber Sellers; Mark Tappen and Colby College.

Editing and Proofreading:
Ben Henning; Chriki Jones; Clara Porter; Kossoma Meach; Brent Wilson; Kate Luddy; Kerianne Kuliga; Kris Hall; and Catherine Fisher.

--The Editors
Cathy Plourde, Meghan Brodie, Elisa Orme, Jack Whelan and Zabet NeuCollins.

...and now, A Word From Our Sponsor

When Cathy Plourde, Director of **addverb** Productions, approached Proactive Resources Design (PRD) to collaborate for a second time on the Out & Allied youth literary project, we were happy to offer our services again! We strongly feel that more people in the gay business community should be donating their time & resources for an underserved segment of gay society: gay youth.

It is a sad fact that in society today, gay youth have very few public role models. Finding an ally & personal advocate is a difficult exercise that may result exposing oneself to ridicule, embarrassment & even physical harm. Therefore, gay youth are a high-risk segment of gay society that should be protected & encouraged to seek out positive gay mentors & allies, and have a safe & non-judgmental place where they can be accepted as themselves and be equal to their peers.

PRD is a proud sponsor and driving force behind the DownEast Pride Alliance (DEPA), a gay business networking event in Portland, Maine, where gay, gay-friendly & young gay professionals can congregate monthly for community building & gay networking. We encourage young professionals to be a part of the gay dialogue and build on the inroads of what older gays have established thus far within their communities. While we cannot cater directly to gay youths per se, once they reach young adulthood, we do offer a supportive & nurturing safe place at DEPA where friends can mix & mingle and be a part of the local gay fabric.

Reaching out to gay youth is as easy as volunteering at gay outreach programs, mentoring gay youth at work, in your church or place of worship, or donating your time & money to gay youth programs in teen centers or with activist groups. Get involved and make a difference in someone's life, you just might save that troubled teen's life and give more meaning to your own. Your community needs you, and someone has to stand up for those whose voice is timid or non-existent. We are fortunate that today our country is a land of many colors, which when put together, form a rainbow. The question stands: How many colors do you want in your rainbow?

Sid Tripp,
President & CEO - Proactive Resources Inc.
Co-Founder of The DownEast Pride Alliance (DEPA)

Introduction

Add Verb's Out & Allied Youth Project — O&A — is focused on creating allies, supporting advocacy, and most importantly, inspiring action. Adding the verb.

Volume 1 has had a ripple effect since its publication in 2011:

- The plays and poems inspired youth to create new works, in new as well as established LGBTQ & Allied performance groups;

- Numerous youth, family members, and friends realized a wider community of support;

- Performance presentations informed how social workers, health providers, artists and change agents thought about how advocacy around gender, sexuality, and orientation could be made fun and welcoming; and

- Volume 1 paved the way for Out & Allied Volume 2!

Our friends at the Religious Coalition Against Discrimination asked us a critical and important question. They wondered if we could bring to light some of the positive stories involving faith, religion or spirituality. These Out & Allied contributors span the Unites States, from Maine to California and a number of stops between. The non-performance sections contain activist tools curated by the editing team with the faith-based communities in mind. We're really happy to point to resources available to help faith based communities better match their values with their actions, and to support individuals and families in their need for a spiritual home and guidance. Not every piece overtly addresses faith or religion, but as a whole they reflect the core values and major concerns of our lives, no matter our age, race, or creed: claiming identity, being true to ourselves, learning from our shortcomings, finding love, and taking action.

Add Verb continues to be inspired by so many who are doing social justice work, but most especially by youth. Change for LGBTQ and other marginalized groups all comes down to youth and youth leadership. Youth are leading the way for significant and meaningful change across the country. Youth activists inspire and lift up other youth, and also inspire adults to step up—at home, school, and places of worship. Youth don't need adult permission to take action, but it sure helps when adults facilitate youth leadership. The results of youth leadership manifest to make things better for all of us, and across all of our communities and circles.

It's fairly obvious but this point is overlooked enough to merit pointing it out: youth leadership is not a young person standing next to the adult and having the adult do all of the talking. Most adults require training to learn how to facilitate youth leadership, and once trained, adults need to audit and inventory their skills. Doing that is a simple process: just ask a young person. They'll tell you where they could have used more support or needed some slack. Creating opportunities for honest feedback is critical to breaking the cycles of power and privilege.

Add Verb would like to acknowledge all people who strive to match their values with their actions. Congratulations to those congregations—as well schools or theatres or other organizations—which have made a commitment to fostering communities as open, accepting, and free from judgment for their LGBTQ members, neighbors, colleagues, families and friends.

For those clergy leaders (administrators, theatre directors, and activists) who are afraid to take these steps towards equality: please have courage, and know that there are resources and support at your fingertips. It's time.

So get on with your fine selves. Find your people, show your true colors. Learn how to really listen. Check out your assumptions. Put on a show.

Cathy Plourde
January 2014

*"Inclusion works to the advantage of everyone.
We all have things to learn
and we all have something to teach."*
- Helen Henderson

The Role of Religion and Faith-Based Communities

Does acceptance of LGBTQ youth and community members within faith-based communities really matter?

At their core, religious values support rather than oppose equality for sexual minorities: love and acceptance, free from self-righteousness and judgment. Religion is constantly developing; it "lives where it grows, when it is able to maintain its core values while adapting to new facts and understandings" (Michaelson, 2011, p. xx). Across all of the different religious texts, we're called to reinterpret and make space for new ideas when faced with indisputable truths: the Earth is not flat; slavery is not acceptable; and stoning people for infractions against religious or secular laws has no place in the modern world. LGBTQ people are not second-class citizens. Overcoming these interpretive challenges only increases and strengthens our spirituality.

Diversity within faith-based communities is welcomed because numerous perspectives on God, values and how to live a meaningful life, enriches us all. The commitment of religions to diversity and inclusion supports human rights, creates safer communities, and invests in healthier congregations because even shared fundamental values are experienced differently. Individuals and communities can learn from this and each other, because multiple perspectives toward an object or idea enrich and further our own understanding (Michaelson, 2011). Diversity and inclusion lead to growth in the size of a community as well as a deepening in members' spirituality and understanding of difference. Welcoming diversity within faith-based communities creates a better image for each congregation as a whole, thus attracting more LGBTQ members and allies who previously may have been opposed to them.

For a longer and more in-depth discussion of religion, we recommend God is Gay by Jay Michaelson, (2011).

Faith Leaders Working Towards Inclusivity

Do...

- Be intentional with welcoming and affirming messages for your LGBTQ members.
  - » **Suggestion:** Advertise in local papers, on bulletin boards, and in community space that your congregation is LGBTQ friendly.

- Celebrate Gay Pride Month (June) with a special service.
  - » **Suggestion:** Invite LGBTQ members to participate, consider a guest speaker, or maybe include readings that speak to the experience of being a person of faith and LGBTQ.

- Review website and other publicly viewed documents such as newsletters to ensure welcoming, affirming, and inclusive language to move from tolerating diversity to welcoming it.
  - » **Suggestion:** Instead of "...our members include non-traditional families as well as...," you could write, "We welcome LGBTQ Jews, Catholics, Christians, Buddhists, Hindus etc., and their families."

- Review congregational forms, such as membership forms, to always include a fill in the blank option.
  - » **Suggestion:** Recognize that if you live in a state where gay marriage is not legal, you may also have to amend your forms to include, committed relationship or partnered as well as married, single or divorced/separated.

Do

- Celebrate all milestones and anniversaries important to congregants.
Suggestion: Commitment ceremonies, births, deaths, adoptions, transitions, coming out.

- Include youth and work to create an atmosphere of acceptance and safety for them. When your most vulnerable members feel safe, everyone is safe.

- Include specific LGBTQ content in social, cultural and educational programs.
Suggestion: Screening a relevant movie and holding a discussion after is an easy place to start.

- Create a list of local and national resources serving the LGBTQ community and make available to your congregants.

DON'T...

- Assume you know how people identify, their gender or preferred gender pronoun. Take the time to get to know each individual and respect each person's choices.

- Stop. There are always ways to continue deepening your commitment to welcoming diversity within your congregation. Re-evaluate your programs to continue deepening the channels to foster understanding and relationship between congregational members.

- Do it alone. Use your community, encourage youth and lay leadership.

Making the Case for Faith-based Leadership: Notes from the Field

Faithful Passion, Commitment, and Promise: RCAD's Response to LBGTQ Youth

Rev. Marvin M. Ellison, Ph.D., is the Chair and founder of the Religious Coalition Against Discrimination (RCAD). RCAD was founded in 1994 as a statewide network of clergy and congregational leaders from eighteen different faith traditions. Its long-term commitment is to collaborate with other people of faith and goodwill to transform congregations and communities to be inclusive places that honor LGBTQ and other marginalized people. Rev. Ellison, a retired professor of Christian Ethics, speaks widely on ethical issues, including human sexuality and social justice.

To correct the historical anti-LGBTQ bias that has so often been associated with religion, clergy and congregants must now do their own "coming out," this time in terms of shared values and commitment. Faith leaders must publicly make it known that we regard LGBTQ youth as "our own" and as a blessing that enriches us all. Our commitment is to never give up and to continue day in and day out. RCAD will educate to change hearts and minds, promote LGBTQ safety, equality, and inclusion, and advocate for social justice in ways that make LGBTQ concerns visible.

With the exception of public schools, congregations serve more teens and young people than any other institutions in the community. RCAD agrees with their colleagues at the Religious Institute for Sexual Morality, Justice, and Healing, that "faith communities can be places of refuge and support for young people."[1] When clergy and youth leaders are knowledgeable and respectful about sexual orientation, gender identity and gender non-conforming youth, they can be more effective supporters for them. Such support and respectful acceptance literally can be lifesaving for young adults who are isolated, struggling with coming out, and considering how to integrate their sexuality with their faith. As researchers have

---

1   Religious Institute for Sexual Morality, Justice, and Healing, "LBGT Youth" at www.ReligiousInstitute.org.

observed: "Those [youth] who were able to be open in their faith-based communities were also less likely to have considered suicide than other non-heterosexual teens."[2] Upward of 14% of teenagers actively involved in their religious communities identify as lesbian, gay, bisexual, or questioning[3]

Only a fraction of LGBTQ faith-based youth are open about their identities or feel free enough to discuss their sexuality or share their hopes, fears, conflicts, and triumphs with their clergy or adult lay leaders. This situation is not only unfortunate; it is deeply troubling in light of other well-documented facts. LGBTQ youth are too often youth at risk. Four in ten LGBTQ students report that they have been physically harassed because of their sexual orientation or gender identity and expression.[4] Moreover, LGBTQ youth make up 20% to 40% of all homeless young people, many of whom have been forced to leave their homes because their families' beliefs about religion and sexuality prevented them from being accepted. [5]

What all youth need is what every person needs and deserves: respect, recognition, safety, support, and resources so that they, as LGBTQ youth or as their allies, can be visible, vocal, and fully engaged in the life and programming of their faith community. Faith communities have an explicit mandate to pursue justice and peace in all aspects of family and community life, as well as to offer values-based education and counsel to youth and adults. Working toward this necessitates a dual plan of action: attending to the needs of the most vulnerable within society, and eradicating the root causes of discrimination, no matter what our religious tradition may be.

---

2   Clapp, S., Helbert, K.L., & Zizak, A. (2003). Faith matters: teenagers, sexuality, and religion. Fort Wayne, IN.: LifeQuest. p. 100.

3   Ibid., 96.

4   J. G. Kosciw and E. M. Diaz, The 2005 National School Climate Survey: The Experiences of Lesbian, Gay, Bisexual and Transgender Youth in Our Nation's Schools (New York, NY: GLSEN, 2006). p. 4-7.

5   Nicolas Ray et al., Lesbian, Gay, Bisexual, and Transgender Youth: An Epidemic of Homelessness (Washington, D.C.: National Gay and Lesbian Task Force Policy Institute and the National Coalition for the Homeless, 2007). p. 1.

RCAD's Proposed Action Steps

Do LGBTQ youth and those questioning their sexual orientation and/ or gender identity actually feel ready and able to share their joys and concerns openly with their age peers and with the adults in their faith communities? If not, what must we do differently to create the conditions of respect, safety, and support that would make our congregations genuinely LGBTQ-friendly, especially for youth? Our transformative responses might include the following, even though this list is hardly exhaustive of the creative ways in which congregations can act to become genuinely open and welcoming faith communities:

- Make sure that clergy and adults who work with youth are trained and knowledgeable about adolescent development and sexual diversity.

- Provide faith-based, age-appropriate comprehensive sexuality education to youth and adults, and help people of all ages learn how to integrate sexuality and spirituality in ways that are respectful of self and others.

- Adopt a congregational statement of welcome that explicitly acknowledges LGBTQ persons of differing ages and, with their consent, include their photographs in congregational directories and publicity.

- Provide a "gender-neutral" or unisex restroom in your place of worship.

- Use language in worship, preaching, and educational programs that speaks positively about diverse family models and their importance to the community.

- Seek to develop strong partnerships with LBGTQ organizations in your community and participate in the annual Pride parade, Transgender Day of Remembrance, and National Coming Out Day.

- Incorporate LGBTQ persons and activities in all aspects of congregational life and leadership and engage in ongoing faith-based education that challenges the misuse of scripture that demeans or devalues LGBTQ persons.

- Create rituals, prayers, and other ways to acknowledge and celebrate significant life events for LBGT youth and adults, including a congregant's decision to begin gender transition or to change his or her name.

- Schedule screenings of films and documentaries, such as "For the Bible Tells Me So," "Milk," "Trembling Before G-d," and "Call Me Malcolm," and hold discussions about LGBTQ issues, including faith issues. Make sure LGBTQ persons are included in the planning and implementation of any programming so that the congregation is not "talking about" but rather "listening to and speaking with" actual LGBTQ youth and adults.

Do's and Don'ts for Christians

(Adapted from 'My Mind Was Changed' - A Communications Toolkit: A New Way to Talk with Conflicted Christians about LGBTQ People in Church and Society)

Christian-based messaging is important when interacting with conflicted Christians. Conflicted Christians see themselves as fair-minded, but are conflicted when it comes to the parts of the Bible that speak about homosexuality as an "abomination." These ideas result in an emotional and theological tug of war, where emotions and religious values compete against each other. Conflicted Christians want to embrace fairness and inclusion, but worry about what they have been taught in church about LGBTQ people.

Do...

- Know your audience.

- Use personal stories: It can be helpful if straight identified Christians tell their personal stories of how they came to their own gradual acceptance of LGBTQ people.

- Make the Christian-based case for LGBT religious and civil equality.

- Move the conversation away from the secular idea of equality and toward moral inclusion.

- Use clear moral frameworks based on Christian values:

  Inclusion
  All people are welcome to participate fully in the church and in society because Christ welcomes everyone – even those shunned by society.

Love

When asked, Jesus told us that the greatest commandment was to love. Believe that God's love knows no limit. God cares for us all because God created each and every one of us. Nothing God does is in vain.

Judging Not

If someone has been taught that the Bible says homosexuality is wrong, being around LGBTQ people may make them uncomfortable. But despite one's beliefs and discomfort, it is ultimately not for an individual to judge others.

Don't...

- "Proof text:" quote Bible verses out of context to support an ideological point.

  Instead reference how single Bible verses have been used throughout all of history to justify acts or beliefs now universally condemned – the planting of two different grains in the same field, wearing clothes made of two different materials, and the death sentence for those who commit adultery.

- Ignore those who are opposed to your point of view.

  Instead, get to know the arguments, language, and cultural framework from which they are speaking.

Do's and Don'ts for Orthodox LGBTQ Jews

(Adapted from the JQY Orthodox LGBT FAQs: Common Orthodox questions, criticism, and concerns vs. Supportive orthodox Rabbinic Responses[1]).

This provides a platform for supportive Orthodox Rabbis to interpret how common teachings and understandings within Orthodox Judaism are in fact inclusive and non-judgmental toward LGBTQ Jews. Ultimately, being encouraging and speaking out against homosexuality does not encourage or discourage anyone from being gay or not gay.

Do...

- Be open and affirming. Silence just increases feelings of shame and internal suffering that LGBTQ people may experience in the Orthodox community.

- Be realistic. Many of life's challenges are not surmountable. Deaf people cannot overcome their deafness and hear; people who are LGBTQ are who they are, and are free to grow as life leads them. Learn to live our best lives possible within life's realities.

- Realize that many things are considered a toevah (abomination) such as eating shrimp and wearing shatnez (cloth containing wool and linen). Although homosexuality is also called a toevah (abomination), it is a matter between him/her and G-d, and that does not make him/her an evil person.

- Remember that we cannot truly judge a person until we are in his or her shoes.

---

1   Auburn Media, Fenton and Goodwin Simon Strategic Research.

Don't...

- Assume that being out means an LGBTQ Orthodox Jew cannot follow the Jewish tradition of tzniut (modesty) and not publicly discuss specific sexual behaviors.

- Think/assume that being LGBTQ is a nisayon (test) for a person to overcome. A nisayon (test) is intended to bring a person closer to G-d, not suffering to be surmounted.

- Assume that LGBTQ Orthodox Jews have no value or place in Jewish life because you cannot legitimize any of their romantic behavior. You can tell them that it gets better.

Do's and Don'ts for Hindus

As suggested by Ryan NeuCollins, M. Div. and Hindu practitioner.

For practitioners, Hinduism refers more to a way of life than a religion.

Do....

- Realize that Hinduism is varied. There will be many different attitudes regarding even heterosexual activity.

- Realize that supporting and perpetuating one's family and society is viewed as one's moral duty. To this extent, heterosexual lifestyles are viewed as helpful.

- Most Hindus believe sex should be between married couples and should be engaged in moderately.

- Remember that it is generally understood that each person has been the other gender in previous lives; therefore Hindus believe there may be sexual confusion in this lifetime. This often leads to an understanding of sexually different individuals.

- Recognize supporting one's family and community, especially for younger and middle aged couples (referred to as "householders"), is of the utmost importance. Developing one's private, family, and social ethics, as well as assuming responsibility for one's immediate and extended family, are deeply embedded within most Hindus' understanding of religion.

- Remember that Hinduism understands we are different from one another and that we have different yearnings; and therefore there will be a different path for each person.

Don't....

- Imagine every Hindu holds exactly the same ideas, beliefs and values.

- Forget that Hinduism is a broad religion. With over a million gods and four predominant styles of worship, there is plenty of room for divergent opinions.

- Assume that all religious sects within Hinduism view sexuality in the same manner.

- Forget that while many Hindus pursue their spiritual goals with integrity, they are generally respectful of others' rights to do the same – even if these goals differ from their own. Religious tolerance and plurality are two major pillars of Hinduism.

Where do LGBTQ Muslims and Buddhists find community?

In researching how Islam and Buddhism create welcoming space for LGBTQ congregants, we came across various and divergent conversations that were not as developed as they were for other religions. There are big differences among theologies' treatment and inclusion practices of LGBTQ people and, within Christianity, Judaism and Hinduism, what is notable is that the work is happening and has been ongoing for some time.

Conversations about Islam and LGBTQ people are relatively new and not easily outlined in this format. Discussions regarding Buddhism have been going on for a long time, but there are so many different Buddhist practices, the available information is not conducive to the format we created.

We look forward to following how the conversations and activisms progress in the Muslim and Buddhist communities.

Resources:

- Human Rights Campaign: www.hrc.org/resources/entry/stances-of-faiths-on-lgbt-issues-buddhism

- Islam, Gender and Sexuality: www.scribd.com/doc/62798372/Resources-on-Islam-Gender-Sexuality

- Muslim LGBT Inclusion Project: Final Report. Presented by Intersections International: www.scribd.com/doc/71594705/Muslim-LGBT-Report

- Religious Tolerance: www.religioustolerance.org/hom_budd.htm

Living Openly in your Place of Worship:

adapted from Human Right's Campaign
[hrc.org]

The HRC presents a full-length document about living openly in your place of worship. They present multiple steps one might want to consider in the process.

For the full text, with helpful steps in the process of living openly in your place of worship:

http://www.hrc.org/files/assets/resources/livingopenly.pdf

Why be open in a faith community?

• To affirm the whole of you.

• To get the spiritual guidance we need to live honestly, and to let others truly get to know us.

• Living openly allows us to contribute to a stronger sense of fellowship, which enables us to grow spiritually in communion with others, without hiding an essential part of who we are.

• By living openly, you help your community be true to their mission and core values: finding love, fellowship and the divine.

Religious Diversity: Does it Celebrate Difference or Justify Prejudice?

Religious diversity is a term that has long been used to describe both the wide range of faiths present in society today and the intra-theistic differences that exist. Within the last decade, this term has taken on yet another meaning. Some people[1] believe that conservative religious moral beliefs and bias against same-sex behaviors and LGBTQ individuals should be seen as religious diversity rather than as sexual prejudice.[2]

Troubleshooting with Reverend Bill Gregory of Portland, Maine

Q: How do you respond to the interpretation of "religious diversity" as a justification for prejudice?

Rev. Gregory: If one affirms "religious diversity" as acceptable, even desirable, I take the term to mean that in our spiritual journeys, each of us has the right to follow the faith we have or don't have as we deem faithful. One may not comprehend how another can believe what she or he believes. Each of us has a story to tell regarding how we arrived at our present faith position that deserves respectful listening. Listening does not mean agreement, but it can increase mutual understanding, perhaps even empathy.

---

1   For example, Yarhouse & Burkette, 2002; Yarhouse & Throckmorton, 2002
2   Report of the American Psychological Association Task Force on Appropriate Therapeutic Responses to Sexual Orientation, 2009, p. 19 bit.ly/1bzZkrn

Q: How would you approach working/talking with people who may hold this understanding/point of view?

Rev. Gregory: The goal of respectful conversations between people who hold inclusive and exclusive faith systems cannot be expected to be conversion to one's convictions, i.e. winning or losing. A realistic and more justice-birthing goal would be that greater perspective and broadening minds would result for all involved parties. Even that won't happen if the discussion is about abstractions such as principles or others' practices. When the conversations include real people sharing their stories of acceptance, rejection, violence, reconciliation, love, and fear, common humanity will be found. This discovery and acknowledgement are the building blocks of justice.

Rev. Bill Gregory is a pastor currently working for the Woodfords Congregational Church in Portland, Maine. Social justice and spiritual life have been primary interests throughout his life; 34 years as a pastor attest to this. Originally from California, he made his way east, where he has become a regular contributor to the "Reflections" column in the Portland Press Herald. A lifelong student and scholar, he has published two books published, And the Answer is Yes *and* Faith Before Faithlessness.

"And whether you're for gay rights or against them, you have to be concerned about the way our conversation has been taking place. It's been bitter and contentious, with little understanding or generosity on either side."
- Jay Michaelson,
God Vs. Gay: The Religious Case for Equality

Opening True Dialogue

Why do we need to move from discussion to dialogue, and why is it so hard?

If we want to have conversations with people in which we can be respectful and curious about each other and talk about complicated issues, we need dialogue over discussion. Use of the word 'discussion' conjures images and ideas of change, and hope for innovation in thinking, understanding and practice. In reality, however, when people 'sit down for a discussion' or 'hold a discussion' a shift or re-direction in thinking is not usually the result. The etymology of the word discussion may shed some light on why this is so:

- Discussion comes from the Latin, discutere, which means to dash to pieces. It implies dispersion and breaking something up. It is destructive and reductive.

Discussion can be seen as a ping-pong game, two opponents batting a ball, or ideas, back and forth with the intent to win. As fun as it is to debate, it's not a productive means of making change, or furthering understanding. Comparatively, the etymology of the word dialogue indicates movement toward creating a new understanding; it's not about having an agenda or winning:

- Dialogue has roots in the Greek dialogos, where logos translates to word and dia means through.

Bohm (1998) directs our attention to this inference of movement within the word. He suggests the image of a stream of meaning flowing among and through us as a group. It is out of this that new and shared understanding will emerge; shared understanding holds people and societies together. Achieving understanding means speaking honestly. Why is it so hard to talk honestly with each other?

We hold assumptions and opinions about others, toward ourselves, and the world at large. We hold these opinions as truths and when challenged, a person's response is usually to become defensive. To move from discussion to dialogue, we have to be able to suspend assumptions, acknowledge them, and talk about them without attacking each other or feeling attacked. Mutual and respectful curiosity will get you there and it takes hard work and time to do well.

To learn more about Bohm's explanation of dialogue versus discussion, see the full article, On Dialogue (1998), and for tools in how to create space not just for discussion but for real dialogue, see the LARA method on next page.

The LARA Method

The LARA Method was designed in the 1980s by Bonnie Tinker of the Oregon-based group "Love Makes A Family" to facilitate dialogue around emotionally charged issues. The organization closed down in 2009 after they accomplished their core mission to win marriage equality for same-sex couples in Connecticut.

STEP ONE: LISTEN

Often in a debate, when you're listening to your opponent you listen until he or she gets their facts completely wrong so you can use the real facts to make a fool of him or her. Instead, using the LARA Method, listen until you can hear the moral principle from which they're speaking from, or a feeling or experience that you share. Listen until you find a way in which you can open your heart and connect with them.

Try to understand what lies at the core of the question: the fear, the uncertainty, the anger, the frustration, the truth offered by the person talking to you. What might the speaker's voice inflection or emotional state tell you? What assumptions might his/her questions demonstrate? If you know the person, this may help you answer these questions, but it's still important to listen carefully.

What do they really want to know? What is legitimate? If you believe that they don't really want to know anything, but are just attacking you, consider what part of their question might be considered reasonable by others in the audience (or within earshot, if you're not formally speaking to a group).

It's also important to listen to what the person is actually saying. In trying to understand what might be behind the question or comment, we don't want to miss what the person literally said.

STEP TWO: AFFIRM

This is the step we don't usually think about in a conscious way. Express the connection that you found when you listened, whether it was a feeling, experience or a principle that you have in common with the other person. Affirm whatever you can find in the person's question or statement(s) that represents a reasonable issue or a real fear. If you can't find anything, there are other ways to affirm. The exact words don't matter; the important part is to convey the message that you're not going to attack or hurt the other person, and that you know that he or she has as much integrity as you do.

To actually be affirming, this step must be genuine, rather than 'sweet' or 'slick' talking. Generally, it's best to speak spontaneously from the heart rather than to develop 'pat' answers. Share of yourself. This is not a natural process for many of us, but it gets easier with practice.

STEP THREE: RESPOND

We often start here. Instead, Wait. Listen. Affirm. Then respond.

Debaters, politicians, and sometimes the rest of us often avoid answering the question that was asked and answer a different question in order to stay in control of the situation, not lose the debate. Instead, in the LARA Method, answer the question. Respond to the issue the person raised. If you agree with the person, say that too, even if it feels like you're giving up some ground. By doing this, you're conveying the message that you're not afraid of the other person and that his or her questions and concerns deserve to be taken seriously. If you don't know the answer, say so. Refer the person to other sources if you have some or offer to find out the answer that seems appropriate.

Sometimes it seems that the person does not really want information, but is simply trying to fluster you or attack you. Reacting with respect rather than defensiveness or anger is important; it shows respect when a question or statement of this nature is addressed rather than 'blown off.'
Personal insights and experiences often reach people in a way that abstract facts don't.

STEP FOUR: ADD INFORMATION

Step four gives you a chance to share additional information that you want to give the person. It may help the other person or the audience consider the issue in a new light or reorient the discussion in a more positive direction. This is a good time to state whatever facts are relevant to the question the person asked. This may involve correcting any mistaken facts the person mentioned; you can do this now because you've made a heart felt connection and the other person is probably more open to hearing your facts than he or she would have been if you had started there. Some other possibilities include offering resources (such as books, organizations, or specific people), or adding a personal anecdote.

Useful Questions for Dialogue Facilitation

Things to consider before facilitation: too small or too large of a group may hinder participation, and finding the right fit for a facilitator is very important.

Exploratory Questions: Probe basic knowledge.
What do you think about_____?
How does _____ make you feel?
What bothers/concerns/confuses you the most about _____?
What are some ways we might respond to_____?

Open-ended Questions: Not requiring a specific type of response; no right/wrong answer.
What is your understanding of _____?
What do you want to know about_____?
What is the first thing you think about in relation to_____?
What are some questions you have about_____?
State one image/scene/event/moment from your experience that relates to_____.

Challenge Questions: Examine assumptions, conclusions, and interpretations.
What can we infer/conclude from_____?
Does_____ remind you of anything?
What principle do you see operating here?
What does this help you explain?
How does this relate to other experiences or things you already knew?

Relational Questions: Ask for comparisons of themes, ideas, or issues.
Do you see a pattern here?
How do you account for_____?
What was significant about_____?
What connections do you see?
What does_____ suggest to you?
Is there a connection between what you have just said and what _____ was saying earlier?

Cause and Effect Questions: Ask for causal relationships between ideas, actions, or events.

How do you think _____ relates to or causes_____?
What are some consequences of_____?
Where does _____ lead?
What are some pros and cons of _____?
What is least likely to be the effect of _____?

Extension Questions: Expand the discussion.

What do the rest of you think?
How do others feel?
What did you find noteworthy about this comment?
How can we move forward?
Can you give some specific examples of_____?
How would you put_____ another way?

Hypothetical Questions: Pose a change in the facts or issues.

What if _____were from a different_____, how would that change things?
Would it make a difference if we were in a _____society/culture?
How might this dialogue be different if_____?
What might happen if we were to_____?
How might your life be different if_____?

Diagnostic Questions: Probe motives or causes.

What brings you to say that?
What do you mean?
What led you to that conclusion?

Priority Questions: Seek to identify the most important issue.

From all that we have talked about, what is the most important concept you see?
Considering the different ideas in the room, what do you see as the most critical issue?
What do you find yourself resonating with the most?
If you had to pick just one topic to continue talking about, what would it be?

Process Questions: Elicit satisfaction/buy-in/interest levels.

Is this where we should be going?
How are people feeling about the direction of this dialogue?
What perspectives are missing from this dialogue?
Everyone has been _____for a while. Why?
How would you summarize this dialogue so far?
How might splitting into groups/pairs affect our discussion?

Analytical Questions: Seek to apply concepts or principles to new or different situations.

What are the main arguments for_____?
What are the assumptions underlying_____?
What questions arise for you as you think about_____?
What implications does_____ have? (for____?)
Does this idea challenge or support what we have been talking about?
How does this idea add to what has already been said?

Summary Questions: Elicit syntheses; what themes/lessons have emerged?

Where are we?
If you had to pick two themes from this dialogue, what would they be?
What did you learn?
What benefits did we gain today?
What remains unresolved? How can we better process this?
Based on our dialogue, what will you be thinking about after you leave?
Let me see if I understand what we've talked about so far... What have I missed?
OK, this is what I've heard so far...Does anyone have anything to correct or add?

Action Questions: Call for a conclusion or action.

How can we use this information?
What does this new information say about our own actions/lives?
How can you adapt this information to make it applicable to you?
How will you do things differently as a result of this meeting?
What are our next steps?
What kind of support do we need as we move forward?
How does this dialogue fit into our bigger plans?

Evaluative Questions: Gauge emotions and anxiety levels. What is going well or what could go better?

Is there anything else you would like to talk about?
How are you feeling about this now?
What was a high point for you? A low point?
Where were you engaged? Disengaged?
What excited you? Disappointed you?

Naming the Elephant in the Room or How the "isms" Connect

"It is not our differences that divide us. It is our inability to recognize, accept and celebrate those differences." - Audre Lorde.

What do you need to facilitate dialogue? First, a safe space.

What makes a space safe? It's a place where everyone feels welcomed and can participate fully as themselves without feeling threatened or inferior.

Power and privilege are pervasive challenges to honest dialogue and understanding. An important step in the process of facilitating dialogue is to consider potential "isms", (or the large, looming and difficult elephants) that are also in the room. How do we recognize and then deal with the system of unearned advantage people receive on the basis of their identity: race, class, age, sexual orientation,

ability, nationality - all the ways we are identified can also be ways we have less or more privilege by just showing up.

Differences between people impact dynamics and comfort levels. Privilege in any shape or size should be addressed. However, this can be tricky and somewhat daunting because of the fear of conflict and the fear of unpleasant interactions.

People are eager to charge ahead to do good things in the world, but that may mean slowing down sometimes. The traps are easy to recognize if you are looking: An organization is dedicated to youth empowerment, but doesn't have any youth leadership training or youth input for the organization. A volunteer coalition is focused on LGBTQ equality, but forgets to address ways to include people from different economic circumstances, and is blind to the classism associated with who can afford to volunteer and for whom transportation costs, child care costs, or even non-working hours are luxuries.

Confronting oppression is intentional work. Advocates in this line of work must do their own work on racism, sexism, ableism, etc. to discover what baggage they've got in tow, consciously or unconsciously. Bypassing this process reinforces existing oppression and biases. Presumably, people dedicated to social justice know this, and together are nodding heads, "of course, of course". But good intentions, and even good work, don't let any of us off the hook, and we are set up in society to revert to oppressive social norms without even knowing it. Getting called out on a bias is upsetting, sometimes provoking deep feelings of shame and anger.

In our effort to move from discussion to dialogue, we need to push up our sleeves and have conversations about the interconnectedness of bias and oppression, and uncover our individual intrinsic biases. The trick will be in doing so graciously, being willing to thank those who helped point our biases out, and even forgiving ourselves for not catching on sooner. We do this work because change needs to happen, and we believe change is possible — both in others and in ourselves.

These ideas are well-developed in leadership and anti-oppression literature if you want to learn more.

"Leadership and learning are indispensable to each other."
- *John F. Kennedy*

Youth Leadership

Making the Case for Youth-Leadership:
Mash Up From the Field

We asked three talented youth activists, Brianna (B), Maya (M) and Zabet NeuCollins (Z), about their different experiences as Youth Leaders. Here is a compilation of their thoughts:

What is Youth Leadership?

Z: A youth leader is someone who takes action, takes responsibility for that action, and is actively working toward an identified goal. Not only do youth leaders inspire other youths, they are definite symbols of hope and change within a community of all ages and demographics.

B: A youth leader can serve as a role model, a facilitator, or a guide for peers, keeping a group on-task and focused on achieving specific goals and outcomes. It empowers an individual to seek collaboration and action among peers, and this is a highly valuable experience for everyone involved.

M: Youth leadership is one way to motivate other youth to get involved and stay involved in their community. A group that cultivates and trusts youth leadership shows that youth are important and their input is valued: this is very unique.

> "I've think I've met the love of my life: standing up for what I believe in."
> - *youth testimonial*

Why bother with training youth to be leaders?

M: Involving youth as leaders ensures youth are accurately represented and shows the value they have. It shows that the group really trusts youth to put in the time and to develop leadership qualities. Young people often need to see their peers taking an active role before they join in and collaborate. Seeing other youth in charge, making a stand, thinking through issues and trying to have a voice, shows young people that they will be heard.

Sample Training Agendas

Maya Brown and Treva deMaynadier created the STAND UP Action Kit in collaboration with the Waterville Inclusive Community Project. STAND UP trainings focus on creating a safer community, conducive to educating people on the issues and making positive change for LGBTQ youth. Three sample agendas for raising awareness and outreach have been included. Most of the performance pieces are from Out & Allied Volume 1.

For the link to the full document, with the performance pieces included, please see LGBTQ and Allied Spaces, Places and Faces on page 262.

These agendas demonstrate how youth can lead people of any age in a training or activity week.

Sample Adult Agenda

Note: *This training was presented to about 30 adults who work with youth in first through eighth grade in an aftercare program. It was an hour and a half training.*

Introduction
Whole group

Identity Activity Lead by _____

After Breakfast **by Meghan Brodie***
Introduced by _____
Performed by _____

Debrief Questions Lead by _____
  1. Were the parents' reactions realistic? Why?
  2. Who handled the daughter's news better? What makes that reaction better?
  3. How would you react if a student/young person/friend told you he or she was going on a date with someone of the same sex?
  4. What do you think of Rachael's descriptions of gay, straight, and bisexual identities?
  5. Does going on a date "make you something?"
  6. Do you know anyone who is questioning? Is it OK to experiment with dating people? Of the opposite sex?

Vocabulary Activity Lead by _____

The Straightest Gay Man in the World **by Micah Malenfant***
Introduced by _____
Performed by _____

* *This performance piece is published in* Out & Allied, *volume 1.*

Debrief Questions Lead by _____

1. What are the stereotypes that you see in the performance piece and where else do you see them?
2. How do you think the stereotypes would change if the performance piece were written for three girls?
3. Do you think the coach is portrayed realistically? Are there coaches that act like this?
4. Do you think approaching the coach is always a realistic idea?
5. If you witnessed a conversation like this or a student talked to you about a similar situation, what do you think you would do?
6. Do kids who aren't gay get bullied for their gender/sexual orientation?

Data

Handout given out by _____ and _____
Presented by _____

Coming Out Stars Activity

_____ reads script

How to Be an Ally Handout

Brainstorm ideas about how participants can be better allies to their students

_____ and _____ write ideas down on whiteboard

Evaluation

_____ explains

Sample Youth Agenda

Note: *This training was presented to about 20 youth from ninth through eleventh grade in a health class setting. The training was an hour and twenty minutes.*

Introduction
Whole group

Identity Activity Lead by _____

Agree Disagree Activity Lead by _____

Instructions: Have the group stand in the center of the room. Assign one side of the room as "agree" and one as "disagree." The middle of the room is for those who somewhat agree and somewhat disagree. Make it clear that participants can stand anywhere along the spectrum to show how they feel about the statement. Read each statement and allow time for participants to stand in the part of the room that indicates their opinion on the statement. After everyone has moved ask volunteers to speak to why they're standing where they are. Stress to the participants that there is no right or wrong answer to the questions, and that it is important to hear about everyone's individual opinions and experiences. Try to hear from a few people in each part of the room. After brief discussion, move to the next statement.

Example Statements:
1. There are LGBTQ students in my school.
2. I am friends with someone who is LGBTQ.
3. Someone in my family is LGBTQ.
4. I would feel comfortable if someone in my family were LGBTQ.
5. I would know what to say if a friend came out to me.
6. I have heard rumors being spread about someone being LGBTQ.

7. It's really common to hear the phrase "that's so gay" in my school.
8. I would feel comfortable speaking up for someone being bullied.
9. There is a teacher or adult in my school with whom I would feel comfortable talking to about LGBTQ issues.

Facilitator Note: *This activity works particularly well if statements are customized for the group.*

I'm Not Gay But Thanks **by Meredith Lamothe***
Performed by _____

Debrief Questions Lead by _____
1. Why does Marybeth "figure it must be a boy" that Anikah likes?
2. Why do we assume that being gay is bad? Are there good things about being
3. read as gay?
4. Does Joel's attitude about being perceived as gay serve him well?
5. What if Joel were a girl? Would it be a compliment to be considered a lesbian? What are some stereotypes about lesbians?
6. How does Marybeth stereotype straight boys? Are all straight boys like she says? Are all gay boys like she says? Where do these stereotypes come from? How are even positive stereotypes limiting?

Stereotypes Activity Lead by _____

* *This performance piece is published in Out & Allied, volume 1.*

What's For Dinner by **Rachel Beaulieu**
Performed by _____

Debrief Questions Lead by _____
1. What was most important to Dorothy about what her parent was going through?
2. How difficult is it to overcome fears about being rejected if they come out to family or friends? What's at risk if they are honest? What's at risk if they keep it a secret?
3. Why is it hard for parents and teens to talk to each other about their gender, orientation or sexuality?
4. What questions would you have for someone you had known your whole life coming out to you?

Sexuality Spectrum Handout Lead by _____
Spend time sharing spectrums. Put them up on a white board.

Panel With College Students
(Note: For this training, we had college students available to answer the high school students' questions and share personal stories.)

Evaluation
_____ explains

Creating a "Week": Step by Step Guide

Step One: Set a Goal
What do you want to accomplish by setting up a week of activities? Is your goal to educate, to address a specific issue, to make your GSTA more visible within the school, to encourage students to be good allies, or just to have fun? Hosting a week can accomplish any one of these goals, but the activities you choose will depend on your goal.

Suggestions for Possible Weeks:
- Ally Week
- No Name Calling Week
- No H8 Week
- Coming Out Week
- Pride Week

Note: Many of these weeks have websites that are worth checking out.

Step Two: Plan Your Week
Once you have your goal, set up a calendar and start planning your events. Events can take place during the school day, during lunch or breaks, before or after school, or in the evenings.

Here is a list of possible events:
- Two Truths One Lie
- If I Were Another Gender
- Ally Hand Activity - This activity works well if done with separate classrooms or advisee groups and if the posters can then be displayed around the school.
- Day of Silence- For more information on Day of Silence, visit dayofsilence.org.
- Coming Out Stars- This presentation could be done with an entire school at an assembly
- Coming Out Day - Encourage students to "come out" in support of LGBTQ youth.

- Sign an Ally Pledge- The Ally Pledge can be found on GLSEN's website. Have it out in a common area, such as a cafeteria, and encourage students to sign it and pledge their support.
- LGBTQ-Themed Movie Night
- Bringing in a guest speaker
- Make a slideshow - Take pictures of students taking part in the activities throughout the week. Showing these pictures at an assembly or during lunch can be a great way to show the school everything that happened, and it is a good testament to your hard work.
- Rainbow Day - A great way to end any LGBTQ-themed week is to host a "Rainbow Day" where students are encouraged to wear rainbow colors.

After you've picked a few events, a good way to complete the week is to add some final touches. Here are a few suggestions:

- Go into health classes and do a modified training.
- Set up a book display of LGBTQ-related books in the school library.
- Make a poster or display that shows the events for the week.
- Make Ally Triangles which say "GSTA Ally" on them and make them available for teachers and faculty to put on their doors to signify that they support LGBTQ youth.
- Make sure your school nurse and guidance counselors have resources for LGBTQ youth available.
- Have rainbow bracelets, pins, ribbons, or other items available, either for sale or to give away to anyone who signs the Ally Pledge.

Step Three: Plan the Details

Once you have everything picked out, iron out the details of the week. Figure out who will do each task and make sure everything is prepared in advance. Details like printing the Ally Pledge, putting together a book display, presenting to a health class, or running an event all need to be delegated to members of the group. This is also the time when you should check with your administration about your plan for the week. Do you need a special assembly? Do students need to get out of class? Can you put up posters in the cafeteria? Make sure all of these questions are taken care of well in advance. Maintaining a good relationship with your administration is key to making the week a success.

Step Four: Advertise

Once you've gotten the go-ahead from the administration and everything is taken care of, it's time to start advertising your week. Get an announcement in the school newspaper or in an assembly. Put up posters. Whatever method your school uses for getting information out, make sure to take advantage of it. Encourage members to inform their friends that the week is coming up. Students are more likely to be interested and excited for your week if they know when it is and what to expect.

Step Five: Have Fun!

So your week is planned, everything is printed and ready to go, and the school knows it's happening. Now sit back and have fun. Overall the week should be a positive experience. The best way to get other students involved is to set a welcoming and encouraging example.

How to Put on a Performance:
FourEssentialIngredients

It doesn't matter whether you're doing a show or a training, or other event; there are four basic categories to plan around.

People

Use YOUTH presenters!
Know your audience!
Who else should be there?
Do you need a facilitator?

Can you find youth church or drama groups, GSTAs, Civil Rights teams, or other youth leadership groups.

Is your audience "free will" or are they required to be there?

What other agencies, advocates, or resources can help your audience take action in the future?

Do you have a facilitator who can get a crowd talking?

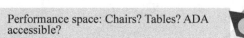

Logistics

Find a space!
Be Flexible.
Organize resources.

- Performance space: Chairs? Tables? ADA accessible?

- Be flexible! Youth time and transportation isn't always their own.

- Organize resources! (scripts, handouts, props, etc.)

- Check your tech. Mics? Music? Speakers? Do a tech run in each new space.

Directing

Do...

- Come to rehearsals prepared.

- Set a good example, e.g. arrive on time, be respectful.

- Be flexible and open to new interpretations and ways of doing things.

- Trust each other.

- Honor each other's confidentiality.

Do Not...

- Be completely self absorbed.

- Be uptight and angry – yelling is never productive.

- Micromanage everything because 'you' know better and can't trust anyone to do their job.

- Assume you know what others are thinking.

- Assume you know better or more than anyone else.

- Treat your audience like they are the enemy

- Assume that what is okay and comfortable for you, is okay for others.

Q & A With Activist and Writer Brianna Suslovic

Brianna is currently studying at Harvard University where she inspires those around her through her passion, leadership, and activism within the LGBTQ community and her commitment to social justice and equality. Brianna was a contributing writer to Out & Allied Volume I and since then, her piece "Run Away" has become synonymous with the anthology. We had a chance to learn a little more about the history behind the piece.

Q: Your piece "Run Away" has become somewhat of a signature piece from Out & Allied Volume 1. What does it feel like knowing your work has taken on this type of role?

Brianna: It's so exciting that "Run Away" has taken on such a major role in the Out & Allied project. I never expected this kind of growth or creative interpretation to come out of my poem, but I'm really happy that it's reached so many minds and hearts. I love writing, and the journey of this piece has been really encouraging and inspiring for me.

Q: I am also really curious to know what it was like to see it performed? Was it what you expected? Did you have expectations?

Brianna: Seeing my piece performed was really an amazing experience. I didn't go in with expectations, I suppose, other than maybe a visualization of a single speaker. To see the echoing voices and movements added to the theatrical interpretation was truly mind-blowing! I was so thrilled to see how much more powerful the piece became with performance elements.

Q: I'm also interested in knowing what was going on in your life right before you wrote "Run Away" – what gave you the push the write such a compelling and powerful piece?

Brianna: As I was writing "Run Away," I was a middle schooler at a relatively small, fairly accepting school. I was still witness to a lot of bullying and ignorance tied to homophobia and heteronormativity, however, and it was frustrating to me that my school's administration didn't punish bullies or provide support for bullying victims. I tried to imagine what the experience of a bullied adolescent would be like, and I also took into consideration some of my closest friends and their very personal experiences with bullying. My school administrators were so lax about these issues that they didn't enforce the bullying policy and refused to support the Day of Silence because it wasn't "age appropriate." The reality is that this issue is of extreme relevance to middle schoolers--middle school is often when the bullying is the worst, and it's also a time of self-discovery for many of us. I really believe in art as activism. I wanted my poem to illustrate the frustrations of someone being bullied in a serious way, and I hope that I accomplished that.

Q: Lastly, do you have any words of advice for up-and-coming and already established youth leaders in having these difficult conversations with their communities?

Brianna: To young leaders: don't be silenced by anyone! Sometimes it's tough to find a kindred soul or a forum for your ideas and beliefs, but never doubt what you feel. It's also so important to find and utilize allies in your journey--they are often able to open up spaces and minds for these sometimes difficult conversations. Since writing this piece, I came out as queer in my high school newspaper, got accepted into Harvard, and I currently study Women, Gender, and Sexuality Studies here. Don't hide what you feel, what you believe in, or whom you love, and most importantly, don't be afraid to express these thoughts and emotions in art. This is a great way to get the conversation going.

"Never doubt that a small group of thoughtful, committed, citizens can change the world. Indeed, it is the only thing that ever has."
- Margaret Mead

How Does
Change Happen

Theory of Change and Stages of Change

One of the most common activist problems? You find yourself preaching to the choir (cliché, but fitting!) How do you help others in their process of becoming better allies? It helps to understand a little about how change happens.

A theory of change is the particular definition you have for your social change drive. It forms the basis for how decisions are made and evaluated, and how progress is defined and measured. It is the means by which you effect the change you wish to see.

Change can be a broad, complicated process requiring different building blocks to bring about a long-term goal. What is the intended result? What's the process of achieving that outcome? Is it the right time? Are people ready? There are many questions to consider which is why having a theory of change can be helpful.

As you work with audiences, congregations, or organizations, a theory of change should seek to answer the following:
- What are your long-term and short-term goals?

- How do you gauge how successful you have been at achieving these goals?

- Through what means will you achieve these goals?

- What is your time frame for these achievements?

These are just the preliminary questions that must be asked. The next tier of questions to consider once these initial ones have been answered include:
- How do you see these changes happening?

- What is your role in making change happen?

- What truths and assumptions do you hold that support your thinking?

- How are you going to get people interested and invested in what you want to change?

Social entrepreneurs, faith leaders, youth leaders, authors, researchers, and activists across the board agree that storytelling and personal narrative are profoundly important. It's the sharing of experiences, feelings, morals, and values that helps people find common ground and a starting point for change!

So, as a change agent, we have one big piece of advice: Pace yourself.

Change, like everything else in life, is ongoing, and in continual development. If obstacles come up, work around them, work with them, acknowledge them, and don't let them keep you down. Once you achieve your goal, keep going!

Example of Theory of Change: From the Communications Toolkit; more information about this toolkit can be found on p. 265.

Theory of Change: The Christian-Based Case for LGBTQ Inclusion and Welcome

To build support for religious and civil equality, we must:
- Make the Christian-based case for LGBTQ religious and civil equality;

- Help Christians work through and ultimately transcend their emotional and religious conflicts with LGBTQ equality in both church and statel; and

Take this new communications approach to the places and spaces where Christians get information – from church pews to newspapers and everything in between.

What works to make change stick?
In general, for a community to progress there are strategies that help—beyond believing that the benefits outweigh any disadvantages. The following is our application of some of the relevant

processes of change[1] with some examples of what the action step could look like.

- **Consciousness Raising**: Increasing awareness via information, education, and personal feedback (Performances, talks, posters)

- **Dramatic Relief**: Inspiration and hope about what good comes from changes (Sharing stories, offering positive examples)

- **Self-Reevaluation**: As individuals or as members of a community, realizing that the change is an important part of who they are and want to be (Aligning with values of love, free from judgment)

- **Environmental Reevaluation**: Realizing how positive effects come by working for positivity (Counting increase in youth attendance, size of congregation)

- **Social Liberation**: Realizing that society is in step and supportive of the change (Offering support to civil rights campaigns and referendums)

- **Self-Liberation**: Believing in one's abilities and making commitments to act on that belief (Standing up!)

- **Helping Relationships**: Finding people who are supportive of creating change (Looking for and engaging with allies)

- **Reinforcement Management**: Increasing the rewards that come from positive change. (Celebrating, honoring, and acknowledging work and efforts)

Stimulus Control: Using visual, verbal and other reminders and cues that encourage positive actions. (Thanking, hugging acknowledging!)

How do people change?

Building allies and increasing inclusivity within our communities can be hard work. In addition to the logistics of using performance for change (For more information on the details see How to Put on a Performance on page 36) there are other forces/barriers at work. If

---

1   These come from Prochaska & DiClemente, 1983; Prochaska, Velicer, DiClemente, & Fava's (1988) 10 Processes of Change. The variables that move people through the different stages of change.

your audience is new to learning about being an ally, it might take audience members longer than just the duration of the performance and post-show dialogue to begin to question their thinking and make new and different choices in terms of their thoughts, words, and actions.

Think back to when you have tried to make a change – maybe you wanted to stop biting your nails, maybe you wanted to go to the gym four days a week. For most of us this required time and practice to make the new behavior stick. Changing an idea or set of assumptions can be just as difficult. Try to recognize what stage of change in which your audience members might find themselves so you can plan your program accordingly:

1. Pre-contemplation: Not there yet, and might not have a clue that something needs to change.
2. Contemplation: Thinking about it, weighing options, pros, and cons. This might take some time, or it could happen relatively quickly,
3. Preparation: Taking action steps — gathering info, allies, strategies, and ideas.
4. Action: Doing something! It's easier to keep up action when you can see how others appreciate it.
5. Maintenance: What motivated you to start doing things differently may change over time — and there are often challenges and setbacks. It's important to have allies to keep moving forward. Sometimes things backfire, and it can seem as though nothing has really changed. Believe you are making a difference to someone!

Even though you may not see or hear a noticeable change in your audience, a seed has now been planted in each person. Over time this can lead them to becoming a fully-fledged ally.

The plays, poems, monologues, songs, and spoken word pieces in this book are here to support you and your community in your efforts to make the world a better place because, as Martin Luther King Jr. states, "Injustice anywhere is a threat to justice everywhere. We are caught in an inescapable network of mutuality, tied in a single garment of destiny. Whatever affects one directly, affects all indirectly."

Performance Pieces

"I wish I could show you when you are lonely or in the darkness, the astonishing light of your own being."
– Hafiz

I

I Made A Boy
by John Coons

I.
I made a boy
and he was
fearfully,
wonderfully
made.
And in his heart,
I placed a gift,
that he would know
the love of Man
and seek it in return,
that it would be
dearer to him than life,
more precious than breath,
sweeter than music.
I made him to Burn.
That through this Love
he would know my own.
And I looked upon
that which I had made,
and saw that it was good.

II.
The boy grew
strong in life, and strong in faith
his face was in my House,
and he prayed with thanks.
He knelt, he sang,
but he did not know love;
his heart was too young
to speak in louder tones.
He sought to live

a pleasing life,
and saw it best to give,
and forgive,
to live, and let live,
to love one's neighbor
as oneself;
Judge not, lest he
be judged.

III.
And then his heart
began at last to speak,
insistent ever more,
and what the boy did hear within
weighed stones upon his soul.
For these words
drawn from his well,
though they were writ with love,
were not as those
from mouths of old
or those that fell
from mother's
or father's tongue.
"That Love is wrong!"
in thundering call
came forth from pulpits high
and family home.
"Should you choose
that path of Love,
surely,
you will be made to Burn."
They were indeed a mighty wind,
and they did shake the ground,
but my voice was not within them.

IV.
And from the depths,
the boy cried out.
With great laments
he called upon my hand
to steal back this gift,
to snatch it from his heart,
that he may be made right,
that he might be good.

But how can one separate
the wind from the air,
the tide from the sea?
How could one
unstitch love from the heart?
He wished to be made Less,
but it is the way of my hand
to make things More.
And all my mysterious ways
left him to sleep alone
among his lamentations.

V.

All comes to all in my time,
to the panting roe
to the seed in the field
and to those who grieve.
And through his pain
the boy did learn patience
and that which was sown in patience
was reaped in wisdom.
The counsel of fools
soon decayed and withered in the sun,
and the boy grew to judge all
by the fruit which it bears.
The harvest of Love
is ever plentiful,
and its insistent voice
weathers all seasons,
all storms,
all trials.

VI.

Then the day came
when the boy saw himself
for what he was,
a clouded glass made clear.
And he saw in himself
a man blessed,
the Light of the World,
the Good News,
the Salt of the Earth.
His heart poured forth
great Alleluias

and the rocks cried out with him
in joy and thanksgiving.
He shared the love of Man
and woke as white and brilliant
as the snow.
And this Love
was dearer to him than life,
more precious than breath,
sweeter than music.
The boy fell mute
in its presence
and knelt,
humbled in adoration.

VII.

The boy lived his days in Love,
caring for Brother and stranger,
Sister and neighbor,
Mother and child,
until the day came
when he gave up his spirit
and returned to the dust.
He came to the house of his Father,
and there he heard my voice,
"Well done,
good and faithful servant."
And Lo, he did rest,
made complete in Love.

VIII.

Only the foolish man would forget
that I am bigger than the Church
or feel fear when faced with love.
Those who would place themselves above Love
shall be humbled by it.
All those that would stand against Love,
its floods shall sweep away.
And to those who would search for me,
I have given you eyes to see,
ears to listen,
and hands to hold.
Seek.
Seek.

It's An Adjustment
by Maya Brown

The night my sister came home with short hair, all my mom could say was, "It's an adjustment." My sister just smiled and nodded and said how it made her head feel lighter. It also showed off her rainbow necklace better. Then she stopped talking about boys. And started talking about girls. That was an adjustment, too.

She never said she was gay. It was just something we kind of figured out on our own. No one really brought it up or asked her. Our family isn't super talkative like that. It just kind of happened. She brought Anna home from college last winter break. She never said they were dating. But they held hands under the table and the pull-out couch was hardly touched in the morning. So we all figured it out pretty fast. And they were really cute together. Anna bonded with my dad about soccer and she even helped my grandmother make the cinnamon rolls for Christmas morning. And they have never tasted that good.

A couple weeks ago, when my sister came home for the summer, she was acting really different. She was wearing even more guys' clothes, and basically had a buzz cut. Her voice sounded like she was trying to make it sound lower, and she laughed when I asked her if I could paint her nails. Then one night, while we were watching a movie with our parents, she reached over and took the remote. She paused it and took a deep breath and said that she had an announcement. That was the night she told my parents she was genderqueer. That was the word she used. Genderqueer. My dad's eyes got really glassy and my mom looked like she wanted to say something, or ask something, or, like, cry at least, but everyone just stayed quiet. Then my sister pressed play on the movie and that was that. I wondered if she was upset that no one had said anything. Because I was. I don't know if I was expecting some huge family bonding or crying session. But I thought her announcement should have gotten a bigger response than that awkward silence.

Later that night I stayed up really late and snuck into my sister's room and woke her up. I basically gave her a heart attack. I asked my sister what genderqueer meant, and we talked for a really long time. She told me that it means that she just doesn't want to identify as either a girl or a boy. And I guess that's ok. I asked her, and she's not trans. She told me that the best way to think of it was that she exists in the gray area. There's man and woman and there's somewhere in-between and that's where she is.

Since then, I've thought a lot about it and I've had a lot of questions. Like if she's gay, too or how all that sexual orientation stuff works. There are some questions I'll ask and some that I probably won't, and I think that's ok, too. I'm not going to pretend I totally understand what my sister is going through or why she feels the way she feels. And I'm not going to pretend that I ever fully will. It's a big adjustment. But I love my sister a lot. So I'm adjusting.

Can You Read Minds?
by Gabrielle Maalihan

Can you read minds? Do you have a mystical ability, or a machine or some righteous power bestowed by the Almighty himself that lets you penetrate my innermost thoughts? No? I didn't think so. So I'm wondering: why you think that you know who I am? I'm wondering why you think you know what's going on in my head. You think you know the intricacies of my thoughts? The endless wonders that make up my psyche? Well, I'll tell you that what's going on in here is beyond your comprehension. In here, it's a festival. A party to end all parties, a hoohah rivalling even Mr. Gatsby's. A celebration of all things me and it is raging on in this house which you may call my mortal flesh. Oh, how you wish you could join. To maybe experience this wonderful thing called me. But this is a party you are not invited to. Sorry, but its exclusive. You see, those who are permitted to enter are those of good heart and tasteful sensitivity. It's only for the understanding, the fabulous and the politically correct. Go and educate yourself, try and de-ignorize yourself. Learn the error of your ways and contemplate. Then maybe, just maybe, I'll let you into this party of *moi*.

A Man Defined
by Sage Landry

Introduction.
Hi.
Luke,
20 years old,
son to my mother,
brother to my sister,
and uncle to my niece.
The usual introduction to me.
I am
a man.
As defined by my genitals.
A man defined,
constricted,
and confined to a form.
A perpetuated idea constructed by
us and you,
he and she.
I find myself challenged by an idea that doesn't fit.
I have laid the foundation on which I stand.
20.
Brother.
Son.
Uncle.
Luke.
Why isn't this sufficient?
It becomes a daily fight to avoid the ideas that don't fit
and at times I feel
I can't win.
When I lose I become
a man of projected assumptions and ideas.
A man who is no longer myself
but a picture of what others presume me to be.

A body for queer assumptions
and gay ideal appeals.
Homo.
Queer.
A gay male of the 21st century.
A man fighting to maintain his own ideas of self.
But instead I become a man confined and oppressed.
I become a man who becomes what you think of me.
Identity, me, is stripped.
Trashed and buried under assumptions and thoughts
of what I am supposed to be.
I become a stereotype of faggotry.
A man endowed with a boa holding a grudge against the 1st and 2nd
quarters.
I don't become me,
I become you.
But I am not you,
I am me.
I am not what you think I should be.
A list of stereotypes that don't apply.
I will never go back around to the man you thought I was.
I am
Gay.
20.
Uncle.
Brother.
Son.
Luke,
L-U-K-E.

Don't Hate Appreciate
by Skylar Addy

I am different...
I'll admit I'm not following the "rules."
I'm supposed to marry a woman.
And have two children.
I'm not like that though.
I want to marry a man.
And adopt three children.

As a pastor I should be straight.
I should be teaching people about how God wants children.
But I am teaching them something different.
My look on God.
He wants us to be who we are.
I mean, why would he make us this way if he didn't?

God is still a huge part of my life.
Though not he nor anyone can change who I am
Some of the other pastors disapprove
I don't care.
I don't hate.
I just appreciate.

I love who I am and I never will change.
I will still go to church
In *my* God's name.

Dad I'm...
by Reggie Stewart

CHARACTERS:
SON   DAD

NOTE: *Fill in the blank with the obvious ethnicity or race that works for the actor and your community, with the goal being to make a joke of what is obvious and does not make fun of someone or something for being other: for example, Dad, I'm black or Dad, I'm a Caucasian or Dad, I'm Asian-Latino.*

SON: Um... Dad? *(Walks up to the edge of the table)*

DAD: Yeah, son? *(Reading a Bible)*

SON: I have to tell you something.

DAD: Can it wait? I'm reading my Bible.

SON: Well....No! It's very important...

DAD: Ok, what is it, son? *(Looks up at son)*

SON: Dad...I'm ..._____ ...*(says it small and quiet)*

DAD: What? Speak up.

SON: I'm _____ *(struggles to say it)*

DAD: I still can't hear you.

SON: I'M _____! *(says it with great emphasis)*

DAD:...

SON:....

DAD: OH HELL NO! *(Slams the book down)*

SON: What?

DAD: Why, Lord? Please, God! Anything other than _____. God! Praise the Lord! Jesus! Mary! And Joseph! It's all those friends at school that got you thinking _____ it's not your fault. Is it my fault? Was the school teaching you about human rights?

SON: Dad, I was just acting.

DAD: I know, I'm just yanking your chain.

SON: I'm actually gay.

DAD: Well, be safe. *(Resumes reading)*

SON: Thanks. Bye, Dad. *(Heads outside)*

I Once Wore Many Masks That Smiled
by Sam Doughty

I once wore many masks that smiled.
Then took them off, just as a child.
Those masks made me, instead of dread,
when inside I was really dead.
I trust myself to live a lie
and never spread my wings to fly.
But the ones that flew where I can't see
are the ones that make the masks of me.
Those masks will smile, but take no breath.
To wear those masks would be my death.

Look at Me
by Duy Anh Truong

Look at me and what do you see?
A nerd, geek, wimp, loser, and every little word you entitle to me.
But at the same time I am more than what you can understand,
I can be anything I want with these two hands but I am also a human
    like you on this land.
You see me as inferior, secondary, crummy, and poor.
But you will see that between you and I, I am superior, the alpha,
    mighty and rich, of that you can be sure.
How I see myself and how you perceive me are two different things.
You see a devil with horns and a sharp tongue but I see an angel with
    a halo and feathered wings.
I don't pay no mind to what you have to say, because I'm still me by
    the end of the day.
I don't care if you judge or criticize me by the way that I am,
because I'm not gonna listen to any goody-two-shoes, wannabe gang-
    sters, or Uncle Sam.
I know who I am, I don't need any help or words of enlightenment
    from you.
You can be this and you can be that but guess what? In the end it is I
    who will always stay true.

Grampy
by Angelica Pendleton

I have several memories of my very early life. I remember being
picked up and put on the counter. I remember lying miserable in my
trundle bed with chicken pox. I remember using the furniture in my
grandparents' living room as a jungle gym on my third birthday. But
one thing I don't remember is a conversation that my mother assures
me took place – the one in which she explained to me what it meant
for my grandfather to be gay.

My grandparents were a proper conservative, religious older couple.
They went to church, grew tomatoes, mowed the lawn. They let my
parents and me live with them while our house was being built, and
they slept in separate beds. It took Grampy several months to build
up to it, but when I was three years old, he officially came out. All
I remember is the yard sale. It was the first time I could remember
meeting my aunt and uncle from New Mexico, and when they left,
my grandfather left with them. My great aunt came to live with my
grandmother, and life moved on.

As I grew up, I moved through stages of understanding about my
grandfather's sexuality. The first was when the rest of my friends
either discovered what "gay" was or when I happened to mention
that my grandparents were divorced (children my age were used to
divorced parents, but they expected it less from older generations).

"What's it like to have a *gay grandfather*?" they'd ask me. I'd shrug and
blankly reply, "I don't know. What's it like to have a straight one?"

I always saw that as a ridiculous question. He was like any other
out-of-state grandparent, so his being gay wasn't important to me,
personally. I knew that being gay was important to other people,
and I quickly figured out that my Socratic response was a good way
of taking the conversation in a direction that didn't lead to me fabri-

cating explanations about my grandfather's sexual identity somehow having an effect on me – it didn't really affect me outside of having to answer other peoples' questions about it.

Later, when my own friends started coming out as gay, I would be there without a second thought, but if they needed someone who could easily ignore the whole thing when they were sick of talking to other people about it, I was there, too. I thanked my grandfather for my ability to see my gay friends and my straight friends as equally valuable.

My grandfather died shortly before I turned eighteen. He'd been fighting cancer since before I was born. It was around that time that I found out more about his long battle with his sexual orientation. He had always known that he was attracted more to men, but his family and church led him to believe that it was his mind that was wrong. He spent most of his life trying to make himself "normal." He got married, he joined the army – and when that didn't work, he tried electroshock therapy and exorcisms. Because of his religion and the society he lived in, he had come to believe that there was something wrong – something cursed, or maybe even possessed – about his mind. He went through many physically and emotionally destructive attempts to "fix" something that wasn't broken in the first place.

I know now what a difficult time that was for my whole family, when Grampy came out. But I don't quite understand it. I don't know what it's like to have a huge emotional upheaval from someone coming out, because "gay" is something that has always existed for me. I suppose it's proof that early understanding and acceptance of those who might seem different is easier the earlier a child is introduced to it. My point of view isn't completely unique, but I have yet to meet many people my age who share it. Most parents would probably consider a three-year-old child far too young to appreciate an explanation about sexuality and sexual orientation, but I disagree. Maybe it's because they learned it after they learned about sex itself, but many people don't seem to understand that telling a child about homosexuality doesn't have to be about genitals and lust. All they need to know is that some men love other men the way Daddy does Mommy and that some women love other women the way Mommy does Daddy; they can make their own genital-related conclusions when they're old enough. Young children are generally the least biased demographic of human society, and explaining basic human equality while they're at that age makes them less likely to become biased later in life.

When I look at all the people my age today – people who are old enough to imagine a family of their own somewhere on the not-so-distant horizon – and I see how many of them support gay rights, it gives me hope. Hope that, maybe sometime soon, there will be many more children growing up who feel as I do. I hope that people will soon react to "My grandfather is gay" the same way they would react to "My grandfather has brown eyes." Grampy had no control over either and I think people are starting to understand that.

I'm a Boy
by Demetri Hernandez

I'm a boy. And yeah I am "trans." Other people call me "butch." People in the queer community have told me that I'm a confused lesbian. I've been called a "tranny abomination" by people I don't know. People are scared of what they don't understand. They don't understand me. They don't want to. I can correct people all day on my gender and honestly, it won't make a difference. I will still get "You haven't completely transitioned"; "You'll always be that to me." I am tired of that. I am tired of defending and educating.

(RISE) I'm tired and (SOFTER) I'm just one person. Sometimes I think, "Where did I go wrong?" I look in the mirror and think, "If only I liked being one of four sisters," and "If only I didn't have to have days where going outside is too emotionally painful because I try my hardest to 'pass' and it's never good enough." But I am good enough. I'm 17 and have a wonderful caring boyfriend who understands me. Sometimes he's the only one I can turn to. I am just one person, though.

Freedom of Me
words by Dreams of Hope and Douglas Levine, music by Douglas Levine

Verse I
"There are no rainbows in hell,"
She said with a glint in her eye.
"Then I can keep my bathing suit on year round,"
was my immediate, sincere reply.
Some use words like a weapon,
afraid of what they don't understand.
But lately, I feel, whatever their deal,
I'm gonna brush 'em off like crumbs with my hand.

Chorus
Freedom of me!
These wings are taking flight.
Freedom of me!
I'm so incredibly light.
Freedom of me!
It's time to soar above my fear,
Time to be strong,
and tell the world that I belong.

Verse II
"I've heard about people turned straight,
so maybe there's some hope for you, too."
"It's better to be somebody who's popping pills
than to be somebody like you."
I used to listen in silence,
to everyone with nothing to say.
But given the choice of raising my voice,
you know I'm raising my voice all the way!

Chorus

Bridge
We're never alone, a single body and soul.
We're thousands together, creating a whole.
So hold up your head when you are heavy with doubt,
and sing the song inside of you that's burning to get out...
to get out.

Chorus

Freedom Of Me

Words by D. Levine with Dreams of Hope
Music by Douglas Levine

Freedom Of Me

As in the beginning

"I've heard a-bout peo-ple turned straight, ___ so may-be there's some hope for you, too." ___

"It's bet-ter to be some - bod - y who's pop - ping pills ___ than ___ to

be som - bod - y like you." ___ I used to lis-ten in si - lence to

ev - ery - one with noth - ing to say. ___ But giv - en the choice ___ of

rais - ing my voice, ___ you know I'm rais - ing my voice ___ all the way. ___

Energetic 4

Free - dom of me! These wings are tak - ing ___ flight. ___ Free - dom of me! I'm so in -

cre - di - bly light. ___ Free - dom of me! ___ It's time to soar a - bove ___ my fear.

Freedom Of Me

3

Gay people are not in the habit of thinking of ourselves as leading our civilization, and yet we do.
- Judy Grahn

Coming Out

Coming Out (All Over Again)
by Proud Theatre

CHARACTERS:
CHRISSIE   LILLIAN

SETTING: *CHRISSIE sits inside the dorm anxiously waiting for LILLIAN to arrive with a table set up with food and candle. She frantically perfects the room as LILLIAN enters.*

LILLIAN: So, why aren't we eating in the cafeteria tonight?

CHRISSIE: I told you, Lils, I wanted to be alone with you… to talk…

LILLIAN: Yeah?

(CHRISSIE is still running around the room frantically picking things up and straightening things out. She begins "violently" rubbing LILLIAN's shoulders as she sits down.)

CHRISSIE: And the cafeteria is super loud and *(Finally sits down with LILLIAN)* I want it to be just us.

LILLIAN: It *is* usually just us. We live together.

CHRISSIE: Well, yeah…

LILLIAN: Besides, food is so much cheaper when your mom pays for your meal plan.

CHRISSIE: Yeah, well, I wouldn't know… besides, you can't pretend you don't get sick of cafeteria food.

(Nervous laughter, brief silence.)

LILLIAN: So...what didja wanna talk about? You're not breaking up with me, are you?

CHRISSIE: What? No! No, no, no. Not at all. Hahaha. No. Where'd you get that idea?

LILLIAN: *(Sighs)* I wish I had this on tape.

CHRISSIE: Well... it's just that I've... *(Brief pause)* I've been thinking a lot about...self identification lately.

LILLIAN: That's good.

CHRISSIE: Yeah, well... I... I joined this talk group on campus... They talk about things like this... and... well...

LILLIAN: Yes?

CHRISSIE: I... I... think that I might be...

(She stops talking and looks uncomfortable. LILLIAN laughs.)

LILLIAN: Chrissie, I think I know that you're a lesbian. Really, I'm kind of counting on it.

(CHRISSIE giggles uncomfortably.)

CHRISSIE: I mean, now that you mention it, this is sort of like coming out.

LILLIAN: What's like coming out? *(Glances at CHRISSIE's stomach)* You're not... pregnant are you?

CHRISSIE: *(Surprised, laughs)* Uhm, no. I don't think I'm in line for an immaculate conception...but I guess this sort of ties in...

LILLIAN: Oh, my God, Chrissie... Spit it out already!

(Brief silence.)

CHRISSIE: I've decided...to re-join a congregation.

LILLIAN: *(Incredulous)* A what?

CHRISSIE: A congre…

LILLIAN: I heard you. A congregation as in…a church?

CHRISSIE: Yeah.

LILLIAN: Right.

CHRISSIE: Lils, I'm serious.

LILLIAN: No, you're not. Come on. Let's eat, I'm starved.

CHRISSIE: Lils — stop. I want to go back to church.

(*Pause.*)

LILLIAN: You're really serious?

CHRISSIE: Yes.

LILLIAN: I'm sorry, I'm just a bit stunned…I guess I thought you'd never go back there, after what happened with your mom and all.

CHRISSIE: That was a long time ago. This isn't about her anymore.

LILLIAN: *(Stares blankly at CHRISSIE)* Oh, my god, you *are* breaking up with me, aren't you?

CHRISSIE: Of course not. Why would you even think that?

LILLIAN: Well, what am I supposed to think? If you're going to go all crazy Christian on me, you may as well just be saying, "You suck, I hate you, get out of my life!" Just like your parents did to *you*.

CHRISSIE: This isn't about you at *all*, Lils! I just miss it, that's all…

LILLIAN: Your own parents wouldn't get a divorce because it was against their religion, so instead they fought all the time and took it out on you!

CHRISSIE: I know…

LILLIAN: And when you came out to them they forced you to go to *Christian camp*. They tried to completely brainwash you!

CHRISSIE: I get that, but that was ages ago. That's not really fair...

LILLIAN: What's not fair is how they treated you. You got kicked out because you were a *lesbian*. I was the only family you had.

CHRISSIE: And you still are. I love you, Lils.

LILLIAN: Then how can you honestly be thinking about going back to church? Your own pastor told you that you were a pervert and would burn in hell!

CHRISSIE: I know...

LILLIAN: I don't know about *you*, but I think any god that would do *that* to someone simply for being what they are isn't worth the pain.

CHRISSIE: I thought you didn't believe in God?

LILLIAN: I don't! That's not the point. I thought you were finally getting over all that shit.

CHRISSIE: I am over it! They were completely wrong and I know that. I think we both know that.

LILLIAN: Then I guess I just don't get why you would ever want to go back. Is this some sort of weird, homesick thing?

CHRISSIE: Of course not. I can't even stand the *thought* of home anymore.

LILLIAN: Well what, then? Help me understand why you'd just waltz right back into the lion's den—

CHRISSIE: (*Interrupts*) Lils! Why are you *attacking* me?

LILLIAN: I'm not! I just don't want whatever weird phase you're in to mess up your life.

CHRISSIE: Oh, wait, so my faith is a phase now?

LILLIAN: Well, this does seem a little spur-of-the-moment, don't you think?

CHRISSIE: Just like being a lesbian, right?

LILLIAN: That's not a choice. Religion is. It ruined your life!

CHRISSIE: Religion didn't ruin my life, closed-minded people did.

LILLIAN: Oh, so now I'm close minded?

CHRISSIE: Of course not…sort of.

LILLIAN: And now you're calling me names! Is that in your Bible, too?

CHRISSIE: You always bring that shit up! Do I have to pay for my past for the rest of my life?

(Pause.)

LILLIAN: Look, I can't deal with this.

CHRISSIE: Lils…

LILLIAN: It's your "faith" or me.

CHRISSIE: What?

LILLIAN: I think you heard what I said.

CHRISSIE: You're really going to make me choose?

LILLIAN: I'm sorry, Chrissie, it's just that after everything I've done for you, everything we've been through together…I just feel betrayed.

(CHRISSIE puts her head in hands; LILLIAN shifts uncomfortably.)

CHRISSIE: I'm not betraying you…I love you…

LILLIAN: I mean…why can't you go to like…I don't know - the Unitarian Universalist Society or something?

CHRISSIE: Lils…

LILLIAN: Or worship the Goddess and North Wind? Even praying to a hamburger would be better! Why do you have to choose a religion that *hates* us?

CHRISSIE: Lils, I'm not…

LILLIAN: I mean, do you really want to be a crazy Bible thumping, born-again bigot?

CHRISSIE: Lils! Would you listen to me? You didn't even wait long enough to hear which church I'm joining or why I'm choosing this.

LILLIAN: What does it matter? They're all the same.

CHRISSIE: Are you listening to yourself? You're being just as judg-mental as the worst homophobe I've ever met! *(Breathes deeply)* Look, I understand you're afraid… but do you really think that I would EVER go to the crazy extremes my parents went to?

LILLIAN: It would be…a bit out of character…

CHRISSIE: You're the one who always said, "Love is never wrong."

LILLIAN: It's not.

CHRISSIE: That's the way I see Jesus and God… as love. Not the way people like my parents or my pastor or Fred Phelps see them. They're just wrong about it all.

LILLIAN: Preaching to the choir, Chrissie.

CHRISSIE: I need *that* kind of love, too. Life is so scary sometimes. I want to be able to pray again. I need to feel like the world is listening.

LILLIAN: I thought that's what *I'm* here for… so you don't have to be alone in this scary world. And I thought…I thought that you were here for me, too.

(Pause.)

I'm obviously not enough for you.

CHRISSIE: Ok, stop it! Look at me. That's not it at all. You know better.

(*Pause.*)

Ok, think of it this way…You go to GSA, right?

LILLIAN: Yeah…so?

CHRISSIE: It gives you a sense of belonging and hope, doesn't it? You feel like you're working with others who are like you, who think like you and want to make changes to the world…to make things better for everyone.

LILLIAN: This is different, Chrissie.

CHRISSIE: It's not. That's exactly how I felt when I first went to the Christian Young Adult Group at the Lutheran Church on campus. I felt like I belonged to something bigger than me. And sitting there, I realized I could talk to them about anything. And I mean *anything*, Lils!

LILLIAN: Yeah, well… we'll see what happens when you tell them about me.

CHRISSIE: They already know about you.

LILLIAN: Oh, really? And they're fine with it?

CHRISSIE: I'm not going to lie. There are some that looked a bit uncomfortable…but they still listened, and by the time I got done talking about how much I love you…I think they got the idea.

LILLIAN: You…told them that? That you love me?

CHRISSIE: Uh, yeah? Duh.

LILLIAN: And the gates of hell didn't open up and swallow you whole?

CHRISSIE: No, silly. Oh, and get this - my new friend, Mary, from the congregation said the sweetest thing ever. I told her about how my parents had kicked me out and she said, "Jesus would never have done that and if they were real Christians, they would know that God always has a plan and that the plan obviously includes gays and lesbians because otherwise why would he have put them here?"

(Pause.)

LILLIAN: Do all your new friends talk in run-on sentences?

CHRISSIE: No…well, most don't.

(Long pause.)

LILLIAN: You're serious about this, aren't you?

CHRISSIE: Seriously serious. I need this. And you.

(Another pause.)

LILLIAN: Well…

CHRISSIE: Well…what?

LILLIAN: I guess…I can work with this. I don't trust religion. I never have. But I can see it means a lot to *you*… and you mean a lot to *me*… so…

CHRISSIE: You mean it?

LILLIAN: (Chuckles) Yes, Chrissie, I do.

(CHRISSIE smiles; she goes over to kiss her.)

CHRISSIE: Like you ever had any real say in the matter…

(Both laugh.)

LILLIAN: But just so you know, if I hear even *one thing* that sounds cultish or ignorant, I'm locking you in the apartment.

CHRISSIE: You know, if you're worried about it so much, you could always just come with me to the services.

LILLIAN: That's another thing. *(Jokingly)* Ever try to convert me and I'll personally open the gates of hell myself and throw you in headfirst.

CHRISSIE: Lils, I wouldn't be able to convert you if Jesus suddenly appeared in our apartment and cured the world of disease, bigotry, and war, all in one day.

LILLIAN: Damn right. I am proud to come out as a hardcore atheist.

CHRISSIE: *(Jokingly)* You? No way!!

LILLIAN: Although it would be cool if that happened. But speaking of cool, I do believe our food is getting cold.

(Both look down at their food and pick at it.)

CHRISSIE: So, you're really okay with me going back?

LILLIAN: I have faith in *you*, Chrissie…and Love is never wrong.

(Fade out.)

Add Verb is thrilled to print these two popular works by Proud Theater-Madison. Founded in 1999 by Sol Kelley-Jones and Callen Harty, its mission is to change the world through the power of theater and the theater arts, and to make a positive difference in the lives of LGBTQ and allied youth through the tenets of art, heart, and activism!

Proud Theater has been nationally recognized for their innovative approach in working with youth in Wisconsin. An incubator for youth leadership and a dynamic/powerful component in statewide efforts to promote LGBTQ visibility, Proud Theater is open to young people ages 13 to 19 who identify as gay, lesbian, bisexual, transgender, queer/questioning (LGBTQ); who are the children of LGBTQ parents; or, who are allied with the LGBTQ community at large. At this writing Proud Theater has three chapters in Wisconsin: Madison, Wausau, and Milwaukee.

Party on Saturday, Church on Sunday
by Proud Theatre

CHARACTERS:

RUTH	JANE
NAOMI	FAITH

Scene I

SETTING: RUTH and NAOMI are talking on the phone. NAOMI and FAITH are sitting in an ice cream shop. RUTH is at her house.

RUTH: Hey, Naomi, I just did it.

NAOMI: Did what?

RUTH: I came out to my mom.

(NAOMI puts her hand over her phone.)

NAOMI: Hang on. *(To FAITH)* I'll be right back, this will just take a sec.

(NAOMI walks outside.)

NAOMI: How did she take it?

RUTH: Surprisingly well! I honestly didn't know how she'd react. I've never heard her say anything bad about gay people, but then again I've never really heard her say anything about it at all. We've just never talked about it, ya know? But she said that God made me perfect, and she still loves me just the same.

NAOMI: That's awesome, Ruth!

RUTH: It really is! I feel so loved and secure, and free now. Ya know...

NAOMI: Don't say it.

RUTH: Naomi, if my mom can accept that I'm gay, then your parents definitely can, too!

NAOMI: They would flip their shit!

RUTH: You don't know that.

NAOMI: I just don't want them to think less of me. I don't want them to look at me differently all of a sudden, like I've become a new person.

RUTH: You're not a "new" person, though. You have always been this way.

NAOMI: *I* know that, but they might not.

RUTH: I'm sure they will understand. *(NAOMI is quiet)* Well, it's your choice, not mine. Since I can't come out without outing you too, I'll wait till you're ready.

(JANE knocks at the door.)

RUTH: Shoot, I gotta go, Jane's here. I'll talk to you later, okay?

NAOMI: Okay, bye. I love you.

RUTH: I love you, too.

(They both hang up the phone. NAOMI returns to the table with FAITH and RUTH goes to answer the door.)

JANE: Hey, Ruth! *(Hugs RUTH)* Were you talking to Naomi? I could hear you through the door. What's new with her?

RUTH: Well, I just came out to my mom, and I was trying to convince Naomi to come out to her parents, too.

JANE: Wow, congratulations! Did she take it well? *(Pause)* Your mom, that is.

RUTH: Yeah, she took it very well.

JANE: That's great! Why doesn't Naomi want to come out to her parents, though? Are they Christians or something?

RUTH: Uhm, I think she's just afraid that they'll react badly.

JANE: That makes sense. But still, I can't imagine staying in the closet. I couldn't keep lying like that. It feels so much better to be honest about who you are.

RUTH: Well, maybe you want to be honest, but you're worried that even if you get along great with someone, there's still that one part of you that they'll reject.

JANE: Like if you love your parents, but they're super crazy religious?

RUTH: Something like that...

JANE: Yeah, that'd suck. Think about all the poor queer kids who grew up in church learning that they're horrible people and going to hell. Man, that'd be rough.

RUTH: Uhm, well, I don't think that's exactly what they talk about in church. Anyway, we should tackle some math now.

JANE: Ugh, I don't feel quite like math right now. Want to walk over to the ice cream shop? We could bring our math with us? It might make this homework less painful.

RUTH: Okay, sounds good.

SCENE II

SETTTING: *NAOMI is inside an ice cream shop with FAITH, one of her church friends. RUTH walks in with JANE.*

JANE: *(To RUTH)* Is that Naomi?

(RUTH looks over.)

JANE: *(Runs across the room and hugs NAOMI)* Hey Naomi! What are you doing here?

NAOMI: Just getting some ice cream. *(Pulling RUTH aside)* What are *you* doing here?

RUTH: We're getting some ice cream while we work on our math homework. Thought it would make it easier to handle. Who knew we'd run into you?

NAOMI: *(Glaring at RUTH)* Yeah, it's a small world.

RUTH: This is Jane.

FAITH: Hi, I'm Faith! It's nice to meet you.

(JANE and FAITH shake hands.)

JANE: Nice to meet you, too.

FAITH: So how do you three know each other?

JANE: We're all in G-

NAOMI: School! We go to school together!

JANE: Yeah… *(gives NAOMI a weird look)* But we're also in GSA together.

FAITH: What's GSA?

JANE: It stands for Ga-

NAOMI: Great School Association! Yep, that's what it stands for. GSA, Great School Association.

JANE: What are you talking about? That's not what it--

NAOMI: So what kinds of ice cream have you got there?

FAITH: I ordered vanilla, remember? Which reminds me, I forgot to get rainbow sprinkles.

(FAITH leaves.)

NAOMI: *(To RUTH)* Can I talk to you for a second?

(NAOMI *takes* RUTH *outside the shop. Everyone inside "freezes."*)

NAOMI: What are you doing?

RUTH: What do you mean?

NAOMI You know exactly what I'm talking about!

RUTH: Listen, I didn't know you were two were going to be here.

NAOMI: We just got done talking about coming out to everyone. Do you really expect me to believe that?

(NAOMI *and* RUTH *"freeze" outside. FAITH comes back and sits down across from JANE.*)

JANE: So how are those rainbow sprinkles?

FAITH: They're great! I love rainbows!

JANE: (*Flirtatiously*) Really now? Me, too.

(*Pause.*)

FAITH: So are you happy with your life?

JANE: Uh, yeah, I guess so?

FAITH: Do you feel like you're missing something?

JANE: No?

FAITH: Oh, okay, then what church do you go to?

JANE: Church? Oh, I don't go to church.

(*Everyone inside "freezes" and attention is turned to* RUTH *and* NAOMI.)

NAOMI: God, I can't believe you would pull something like this!

RUTH: I swear I didn't do this on purpose!

NAOMI: Okay, *sure.* Whatever you say.

RUTH: Naomi, I swear to God I didn't! Besides, they probably won't even figure it out…I hope.

NAOMI: Yeah, right! Knowing Jane she'll probably hit on Faith! How on Earth are we going to explain that?!

(RUTH and NAOMI freeze and attention switches back inside.)

FAITH: They sure are taking a while.

JANE: I wonder what they're talking about.

FAITH: It kinda looks like they're fighting.

JANE: I wonder why.

FAITH: Hmmm…

(Pause.)

JANE: Anyway, you're kinda cute.

FAITH: Oh, uhm, thanks. You're pretty, too…

JANE: So are you seeing anyone? *(Puts her arm around FAITH's shoulder)*

(Everyone inside "freezes" and attention is switched back to outside.)

NAOMI: They're probably wondering why we've been out here so long.

RUTH: Yeah, we should probably go inside.

NAOMI: God, I hope they didn't figure it out yet!

(NAOMI starts to leave, but RUTH stops her.)

RUTH: Naomi, wait a minute. Can we just stop for a second? I mean, listen to yourself. Do you want to be like this, constantly worrying about being outed? Because I don't. I know that it's scary, but being truthful with our friends will outweigh any fear that you have now.

NAOMI: Ruth, you don't know how terrifying this is to me! I don't want to lose any of our friends over being Christians or being lesbians!

RUTH: You don't think I'm just as scared as you are? I don't want to lose friends either, but if they can't like us for who we really are, then we shouldn't hide that part just to be friends with them.

(Long pause.)

NAOMI: I guess...I guess you're right.

RUTH: And remember, you're not in this alone. We have each other. *(They hug)* But now we should really get inside. I can see Jane is all over Faith.

NAOMI: Oh, crap!

(NAOMI bolts in and removes JANE's arm from FAITH's shoulder.)

NAOMI: Jane! Stop! We have something to tell you. Ruth and I kind of go to church with Faith.

JANE: What?

RUTH: We're Christians and we go to church.

FAITH: Why would she care about you going to church? Don't most people?

NAOMI: Faith, the reason we didn't tell her is because...is because... because she's a lesbian.

FAITH: Oh.

NAOMI: And so are we.

(Pause.)

FAITH: Oh. Wow. Uh, this is a lot to take in. I , uh...I need to step outside and get some air for a minute.

RUTH: Faith, wait!

(FAITH exits.)

JANE: So, you two are Christians?

NAOMI & RUTH: Yes.

JANE: Well, I knew that you both went to church. I mean, come on. Visiting our inspirational speaking carpenter Uncle Jesus every Sunday kinda gave it away. So why didn't you make it clear that you were religious?

RUTH: Because you always made all those mean jokes about Christians.

JANE: The only reason I made all those jokes is because I thought your parents forced you to go, like it wasn't your choice.

NAOMI: Yeah, well, we go because we want to.

JANE: Oh, okay. I'm sorry for being a jerk before. So long as you don't try and convert me, I'm sure I'll get over it.

NAOMI: Thanks, Jane.

(Pause.)

JANE: Sure thing. But you better make sure your friend is okay — she seemed a little freaked. *(Pause)* She's really hot.

NAOMI: We will. See you later, Jane.

RUTH: Yeah, I'll be back in a few.

(RUTH and NAOMI step out and find FAITH.)

RUTH: Hey, is everything okay?

FAITH: Yeah, yeah, I'm fine. It's just...that's a big thing to tell someone. Not to mention your friend hitting on me.

NAOMI: Yeah, sorry about that.

RUTH: We usually keep a better eye on her.

(Awkward laughter, then a slight pause.)

FAITH: So why didn't you guys tell me before?

NAOMI: Because you are always saying stuff like "That's so gay" and always seem uncomfortable when you're around queer people. We thought you wouldn't want to be around us if you knew we were lesbians.

FAITH: Oh, um, wow. *(Pause)* I could never hate either of you, though. You know that, right?

RUTH: Yeah, we know.

(Slight pause.)

FAITH: I'm sorry. I don't really know what to say.

RUTH: Do you wanna just go back inside?

(Lights shift to ice cream shop interior. All three go back in and sit down; Beat.)

JANE & FAITH: So....

(Slight pause; lights fade to black.)

Let Me Be Me

by Kaitlin Hunter arr. by Douglas Levine for Dreams of Hope

Every day I walk down the street
People making judgments of me
Like they know my story, but they only know what they see.

Never knowing what's inside
Before they go and turn a blind eye
If they'd only try, they'd know there's no way to deny-

Chorus
I am not the clothes that I wear
I am not the way I wear my hear
I am not this skin
So let me come in
And let me be me.

I choose not to fit the mold
That our mad society holds
Cause I'm sick of being told, that I'm leaving my morals in the cold.

I am not some stereotype
So please don't believe the hype
Don't let my hopes die, because I am ready to fly.

Chorus 2x

I am not this skin
So let me come in
And let me be me.

Let Me Be Me

Words & Music by Kaity Hunter
Arranged by D. Levine

Let Me Be Me

What's For Dinner?
by Rachel Beaulieu

CHARACTERS:
DOROTHY, daughter   JESS, biological father of DOROTHY
SADIE, stepmom

DOROTHY: *(Writing, reads out loud)* What made you decide you wanted to be a woman instead of a man?

(Pauses, thinks, reads out loud.)

What do you think will make becoming a girl better than staying the same?

(Pauses, thinks, reads out loud.)

How long have you been thinking about this?

(To audience.)

So, it turns out my dad wants to be a female. My stepmom, Sadie, was the one who told me because my dad doesn't like to say personal stuff out loud, which is the same for me. So after Sadie told me, she asked me to go upstairs and write down any questions I had. I thought about it for a little bit, and just sat there. I have been noticing Dad growing his hair out more and getting his ears pierced. I didn't really have any questions because as long as my dad is happy, I can be happy. But I wrote some down because I didn't want them to think I was ignoring the whole thing.

JESS: I really hope Dorothy can understand why I am doing this. If she has any questions, then I can answer them. The biggest fear I have is rejection from the people that I love. I don't want her to feel like she is losing a father. I have been dressing as a woman for a few months, but not around Dorothy. But Sadie pushed me to tell Dorothy. She said, "Look, this is your daughter and you need to be honest with her." I didn't want Dorothy to just storm off or ignore me or hate me.

DOROTHY: *(Crumples paper. Silently writes question on a new sheet of paper.)* I went back downstairs. My dad and Sadie were sitting in the living room watching TV with the cat. I snuck up behind the couch and said, "Boo!" They were so freaked out that they scared the cat, who started clawing their legs.

JESS: All right, goofball. What questions do you have?

(DOROTHY, still standing behind the couch, hands the paper to JESS.)

ALL: What's. For. Dinner?

(They all laugh, and have a group hug.)

DOROTHY: But really, what's for dinner?

Team Player
by Alissah Paquette

CHARACTERS:

BEN, son (gay)   MOM, Ben's mom

SETTING: *BEN and MOM are in the car, driving home from a baseball game.*

NOTE: *Stage and blocking is important.*

(BEN and MOM enter onto the stage, leaving the baseball game and getting in the car.)

MOM: Good job today! You really stepped it up and played as a team.

BEN: Mom, can I talk to you about more of a personal topic?

MOM: Of course you can.

BEN: Well, for a while now I've wanted to tell you, I think I'm gay.

MOM: Oh…well, there's no problem with that.

BEN: Really? Aren't you going to get mad at me or ground me for life?

MOM: Why would I? Love is love. *(Pauses)* But Ben, why did you choose to tell me now?

BEN: I haven't slept, I haven't been hungry, I can't have fun, and all of my grades have dropped. It has been like this for the last couple of weeks.

MOM: Why didn't you tell us sooner?

BEN: I tried, but I just couldn't do it.

MOM: Well, I am glad that you came out and told me. Will you promise that no matter how busy your dad and I are, we will always be truthful with you as long as you be truthful with us? That you will tell us anything that is going on in your life and we will be more connected in yours as well?

BEN: Always.

MOM: No more secrets.

BEN: No more secrets.

Three Ways to Tell Your Mom
by Megan E. Tripaldi

CHARACTERS:
GIRL   MOM

SETTING: An empty stage.

AT RISE: A GIRL stands at center. Off to the side, sitting in a chair reading is her MOM. GIRL addresses audience.

GIRL: Hello, hi, um…Thank you for having me here with you today. I know we just met, but at this time I'd like to tell you all something very personal about myself: I'm bisexual. Wow, that was easy. It's because you're complete strangers, right? Right. But my mom? That's a whole different story. See…I need some help, um…I'm trying to come out to her, and nothing, I mean *nothing* seems to work in my head. Why now? Well, why not now. I've known for a really long time, I just…I hate having secrets with her. And don't get me wrong, she's not a bad person, it's just…it's really hard to picture a reaction for this sort of thing…you know? Can…can I give you examples? Really? Awesome! I call this one: It's All About Me.

(*She turns to her* MOM.)

Mom?

MOM: Yes, honey?

GIRL: I have to tell you something.

MOM: Well, what is it, sweetie? I'm all ears.

GIRL: Mom, I'm…I'm bisexual.

MOM: What? What does that even mean?

GIRL: Well...it means I'm attracted to girls and I'm attracted to guys.

MOM: You can't be attracted to both, that doesn't even make sense.

GIRL: Well, it's more of a...I love who I love kind of thing, you know?

MOM: So, what, if you fall for a girl, that makes you a lesbian?

GIRL: No, I -

MOM: And if you fall for a boy, you're straight again?

GIRL: No, mom, listen -

MOM: I don't understand you. Are you doing this for attention? Is it because I forgot about your soccer game?

GIRL: It was hockey, mom...

MOM: You are just trying to hurt me, aren't you?

GIRL: No, mom, this isn't about you!

MOM: Am I really that bad of a mother?! Why do you hate me?!

GIRL: I don't hate -

MOM: Go! Get out of here! Out of my sight!

(MOM goes back to reading. GIRL turns back to the audience.)

GIRL: Did you see that? That sucked! My mom is usually pretty cool, but you never know. Announcing something like this brings out weird feelings in people sometimes and even weirder reactions. My friend's dad, liberal as they come, he came out to him and he just cried...for like, hours. It was awful. But I shouldn't just think this way, right? This situation doesn't always generate negative reactions, you know? For example, my second scenario is called: Ten People I Know Facts About So I Don't Have to Confront The Fact that My Daughter is Pouring Out Her Heart to Me. Let's watch! *(She turns back to MOM.)* I'm bisexual.

MOM: Wow...

(Pause.)

You know your Uncle Jimmy's best friend's sister was a lesbian.

GIRL: Okay...

MOM: And there was this couple once, such a cute couple. They were these homosexual men I saw on the subway...

GIRL: Mom...

MOM: And you know everyone has that experiment phase in college...

GIRL: Mom!

MOM: Well, not me, but my roommate was a very...sexual person. And she had this one girl over -

GIRL: I don't need to hear this!

MOM: She was friends with a couple of men who went to those leather bars –

GIRL: (Puts fingers in ears) La la la la la...

MOM: And of course, everyone makes out with a couple of gay men at those theatre parties...

GIRL: MOTHER!

MOM: Maybe I should introduce you to my boss' sister's daughter. I think she's an art student...

GIRL: STOP!

(MOM goes back to reading. GIRL turns frantically to the Audience.)

Oh my goodness, that was horrifying! What was I thinking, I can't do this... I might as well just stay in the closet; this is too freaking hard...

(*MOM gets up and approaches GIRL.*)

MOM: Are you okay, sweetie?

GIRL: What, me? No, I'm fine. Just great. (*Beat.*) No, I'm not fine. I need to tell you something.

MOM: Well, what is it, sweetie? I'm all ears.

GIRL: Mom...I'm, uh...I'm...

MOM: Take your time, honey. Whatever it is I'm sure it's nothing bad.

GIRL: I hope not...Ok, I can do this. Mom, I'm...bisexual.

(*Beat.*)

MOM: Okay.

GIRL: What? Okay?

MOM: Okay.

GIRL: No twenty questions, no guilt? Just...okay?

MOM: Whoever you are is ok with me. As long as you're being yourself and that makes you happy, then I'm happy, too.

GIRL: Really? Wow... Thank you, mom.

MOM: You're welcome, honey. I love you.

GIRL: I love you, too.

(*They embrace. MOM exits.*)

Wow...I did it!

(Blackout.)

Before She's Gone
by Skylar Addy

CHARACTERS:

JENNA   MARISSA   MARISSA'S MOTHER

NOTE: *When one person is doing their line all the others freeze, unless the line is for all characters.*

ALL: I don't know what to do

JENNA: Yesterday Marissa told me that she was a lesbian. How could she? We've been friends for years. It has always been Marissa and Jenna, inseparable. What if she's had some sort of crush on me for this long? Do you know how many times I've changed in front of her? When she came out to me I didn't know what to do. So I ran. I can't be seen with her anymore. What if people start to think that *I'm* a lesbian? On the other hand, she has been my friend forever, and if she ever wanted to come on to me, she would have already—right? I am not into all that "lesbo" stuff! Before you know it she'll cut all her hair off and stop shaving! Gross!

ALL: My heart is broken.

MARISSA: I can't believe how Jenna took it. It wasn't like I was going to be any different. Maybe happier, but that's not bad! This was not supposed to affect our relationship or turn her away! She has left me with no one! Soon everybody will know who I am! *What* I am! My church will disown me! My family! What am I supposed to do now?

ALL: I can't believe myself.

JENNA: *(Looks down at her bracelet)* Marissa made me this bracelet when we were in kindergarten. Oh. My. Gosh. What have I done? How could I be scared of being around my best friend? Who am I? Who do I think I am? I have to go back. I have to help her through this. How can I live with myself if she hurt herself because of me?

ALL: I don't know what to do.

MARISSA: What happens when Jenna tells everybody? What if people start to hate me? I have to leave. I can't stay here anymore.

(MARISSA turns around so her back is to the audience.)

JENNA & MARISSA'S MOTHER: My heart is broken.

MARISSA'S MOTHER: *(Crying)* My little girl. How could she leave me like this? Without a reason? Grabbed her shoes and ran. How can I live with myself not knowing why she ran? Am I a bad mother? I know times have been rough with her father leaving and everything, but I've tried my best and done all that I can do. She was supposed to be at Jenna's! When I called her for dinner, Jenna said she had never been there! Did she bring money? Her cell phone? Oh, I just hope she will come home!

JENNA & MARISSA'S MOTHER: I can't believe myself.

JENNA: She is gone? Before I could apologize! I couldn't believe it when her mother called me! Ugh! I can't believe I was too late. How could I let this happen to her?

(MARISSA turns back around to face the audience. JENNA and MARIS-SA'S MOTHER turn around, their backs now to the audience.)

ALL: I can't do this.

MARISSA: I can't hurt them like this. I want to go back home. I need to go back. *(Pauses)* I'm afraid to go back.

(MARISSA'S MOTHER and JENNA turn back around to face the audience and they all join in for a group hug.)

ALL: I love you.

Coming Out: What Not To Do
by Maya Brown

CHARACTERS:

ANNOUNCER   QUEER PERSON   OTHER
PERSON

NOTE: *ANNOUNCER'S lines can be played by QUEER PERSON, who will then just step out and back into the scene.*

ANNOUNCER: Hello everyone. Today's topic is disastrous coming out stories. Want to know what happens when you come out? Well, there's a range of ways it can go. So I've broken it up into some handy categories for you. First up, there's the Over-ReACTOR...

QUEER PERSON: Hey, you know I'm gay, right?

OTHER PERSON: WHAT? OH MY GOD, OH MY GOD OH MY GOD CAN WE TALK ABOUT THIS? THIS IS LIKE A THING WE SHOULD *PROBABLY* TALK ABOUT. OK SERIOUSLY THIS IS SUCH A BIG THING. AHH! I CAN'T EVEN HANDLE IT. I CANT EVEN.

ANNOUNCER: Then there's the opposite. The Under-ReACTOR, if you will...

QUEER PERSON: I have something I want to tell you. It's like a pretty big thing and I've wanted to tell you for a long time. So I'm just going to come out and say it, ok? I'm gay.

OTHER PERSON: Oh yeah, I knew that. Like, everyone did. What's the algebra homework?

ANNOUNCER: Next up, the person who wants to become your therapist…

QUEER PERSON: So, I need to tell you something. I'm a lesbian.

OTHER PERSON: Really? Thank you *so much* for telling me. When did you first know? Has it been hard? Are you like, telling other people? Do your parents know? Are they ok with it? Wow, this must just be, like, so hard for you. But don't worry. I'm totally here for you. Do you have a lot of feelings? I'm sure you have like, so many feelings. Let's work through your feelings together. With me. Go ahead. Talk. Together. Feelings.

ANOUNCER: Or the other person may be one of those One-Uppers…

QUEER PERSON: Hey, I've been doing a lot of thinking, and I think I might be bisexual.

OTHER PERSON: Wow, that's pretty big, but *guess what*? My sister is *pregnant*! She like just told my parents and they are freaking out. I mean she's engaged, but still, like, she's barely out of college! I think they'll come around eventually but like oh my god, do you want to see her sonogram? I hope it's a boy.

ANNOUNCER: And the One-Upper is not to be confused with the Collector…

QUEER PERSON: Just so you know, I'm gay.

OTHER PERSON: Oh, my cousin just came out too. I'm pretty sure my neighbors are gay, or maybe they just live together, and I think our elementary art school teacher is gay, did you know that? Mr. Simon, yeah. I swear that guy wasn't just his friend; they held hands way too much for that. Hmm, I also have a friend from summer camp who's a lesbian, if you wanted me to introduce you I totally would, but I think she might be dating someone. And also, I haven't told anyone yet but I think my cat is bi; she like totally has a thing for my aunt's cat, and they're both *girl cats*. A lot of TV shows I watch have gay people. I love gay people! I know so many!

ANNOUNCER: Or, there's the one who wants too much information: The TMI Guy.

QUEER PERSON: So, you know Michael/Sally, right? Well, we've started dating, and it's going really well!

OTHER PERSON: Wow! Okay. (Pauses) So can I ask you a couple of questions...like some awkward question...so how do you...you know...I mean have you...and does, *that* like, *count?* I mean what do you do for...and do they...and how do you do *that?*

ANNOUNCER: Then there's the Stereotypist...

FEMALE QUEER: I'm a lesbian!

OTHER PERSON: Oh. Wait. Are you going to cut off your hair? Do you play rugby? Will you stop shaving now? I'll trade you my brother's old plaid flannel shirts for your dresses — you guys are pretty much the same size... I don't really want to watch the *L-Word*, but if you want, I'll do that with you.

MALE QUEER: I'm gay!

OTHER PERSON: Oh — It all makes sense now! You're so into musical theatre and you're *such* a good dresser! So does this mean you can be my shopping buddy now? *Puhlease* be my shopping buddy. But you can't start having better fashion sense than me, ok? Wow, this is so exciting; I have seriously always wanted a sassy gay best friend! Let's have a Glee party, and you can do my nails!

ANNOUNCER: Okay, okay, you get the idea. It can get pretty crazy.

(QUEER PERSON steps forward.)

QUEER PERSON: Yeah, and these are the supportive ones, even if they didn't get it quite right. For some it can get a lot worse.

ANNOUNCER: Here's a sampling.

(QUEER PERSON steps back, OTHER PERSON turns to face audience.)

OTHER PERSON: There's a cure. It's a phase. I'll pray for you. We can fix you. You're just confused. You chose this lifestyle. I bet you have a crush on me. How could you do this to me? I can't be your friend. *(ACTORs pause.)*

ANNOUCER: What is the right thing to say?

(QUEER PERSON steps out.)

QUEER PERSON: Sometimes it's nothing at all.

(QUEER PERSON steps back and faces OTHER PERSON.)

QUEER PERSON: I have to tell you something. I'm gay.

(OTHER PERSON takes it in, and gives QUEER PERSON a hug.)

"*I learned a long time ago the wisest thing I can do is be on my own side, be an advocate for myself and others like me.*"
-Maya Angelou

Learning Curve

What's In a Name (Excerpt)
By Karl O'Brian Williams

CHARACTERS:
CAMILLE   BARBIE

CAMILLE: It's fine, James, you can tell me. I mean, come on, you know I've only got like one friend, and we don't talk about other people, we're sort of in our own world. I mean, you said it, I'm weird, right?

BARBIE: I'm sorry I didn't mean that, it's just what I've heard people say about you…

CAMILLE: Really, what else do they say?

BARBIE: Nothing. Just that you're weird, and you do weird stuff. I'm ok now, I just had a fight with a fr – former friend of mine at the Gallery – it was pretty embarrassing.

CAMILLE: Sorry to hear that, friendships are tough you know. Did your friend do something to hurt you?

(No response)

CAMILLE: Hey, people say all kinds of things, but it doesn't matter; it never matters what they say.

BARBIE: Yes, it does. It does matter what they say, and it matters what they call you. and what they think about you, and if you don't believe that, you're lying to your self.

CAMILLE: You really believe that?

BARBIE: Yes!

CAMILLE: That's surprising, coming from you.

BARBIE: What is that supposed to mean?

CAMILLE: I mean, come on, you're in drag. Surely you must know how they feel about that stuff in our neighborhood, in your own house. I mean James, even your brother's a homophobe. He embarrassed you last year near the park – everybody heard — so how can you say you care what people think and then be so, so...

BARBIE: So I don't choose to be boring like you and sit and take what they have to say. And disappear behind the shelves of a library and possibly have a million cats...

CAMILLE: I have one cat!

BARBIE: Whatever. I'm me, Barbie, and when I don't choose to be Barbie, I'm James, and even though they say shit about me, they will always see me. I am not gonna be invisible!

CAMILLLE: But you won't always be safe.

BARBIE: Are you safe? Who wants to be safe? I want to be remembered. And you talk about my brother and me, but my brother doesn't even know you exist. He's away in college now, anyway, so I don't have to worry about him.

CAMILLE: He pretended not to know I existed. I had just as many medals as he did in high school; but, see, it doesn't matter! Both of us sports champions – and yet, I'm still the "weird one."

BARBIE: No, see it does matter, because people like my brother are still being spoken about by people like you, who no one talks about, except when they're being made fun of. I've got my spaces where I go and people love me. Where do you go to be loved?

Writer Karl O'Brian Williams is a playwright, ACTOR, director, and teacher originally from Kingston, Jamaica, living in Brooklyn, NY.

The Theatre Askew Youth Performance Experience (TAYPE), under the direction of Askew artistic director, Tim Cusack, provides a safe, creative forum to develop and empower the unique voices of LGBTQ youth. In addition to theatrical training, youth are introduced to the New York theatre world, including working theatre artists who can inspire, guide, and serve as role models.

What's in a Name was developed over a 6-month process of acting improvisations, compositional work, writing prompts, and group discussions centered around questions of self-naming, labeling of others, and stereotypes. It premiered at the Ohio Theatre on Christopher Street in New York's West Village neighborhood on May 23, 2012. The roles of Camille and Barbie were played by Gail (Henry) Schreibman and Tommy Kis.

Joining our production team for What's in a Name was a past TAYPE participant who now attends Brooklyn College. This young woman comes from a very socially conservative family: immigrant (Latino/German) and devoutly Catholic. When Mariaisabel first joined us in 2009, she was a classical voice major at La Guardia Performing Arts High School (the "Fame" school). Her parents were not exactly thrilled that their ostensibly straight child, who was being groomed for a mainstream opera career and who earned money as a soloist at their parish church, would be associated with an alternative queer youth theatre. When they came to see the production their daughter performed in, it was tense.

Two years later, they came back – even though Mariaisabel wasn't performing but rather assisting behind the scenes. Their change was palpable. Her mom asked two amazingly insightful questions of the cast during the post-performance talkback. Afterwards, she told me that Mariaisabel's participation in the program had changed her life and that's why they wanted to show their support for the program by coming to see other people's kids perform. But clearly her daughter's experiences had transformed her deeply religious family as well.

Guidance
by Izzie Szatkowski

CHARACTERS:

TAYLOR a teenage girl   JONAH, a friend of hers
GUIDANCE COUNSELOR   TEACHER

TAYLOR: *(To audience)* There were two different possible reactions running through my head when I first started telling people that I was bisexual. The first was that it was a phase and I would get over it soon. After all, who doesn't like to be promised that one day they'll be living the American dream, married to a guy with a two car garage and 2.5 kids? And the second was 'I love you no matter who you are.' Which really explains itself. I wasn't sure which I would have liked to hear, but at the time I didn't have a choice and was told both.

(TAYLOR turns and sits down at a table across from a woman in her mid fifties.)

TAYLOR: *(To audience)* Reaction number one:

GUIDANCE COUNSELOR: So what can I help you with today Taylor? Friendship problems? Parent issues?

TAYLOR: *(Looking confident)* Well, actually I do have a friendship problem but to be completely honest with you so you can help me I need you to know something about me. *(Pauses)*

GUIDANCE COUNSELOR: It's okay Taylor, you can tell me anything, I'm here to listen.

TAYLOR:….I'm bisexual.

GUIDANCE COUNSELOR: *(Looking very uncomfortable)* Oh, well then. You do know everyone goes through phases such as these and you will get over it? It's not natural, Taylor. Anyway, what were you saying about your friend?

(COUNSELOR freezes, TAYLOR gets up and walks across to where JONAH is sitting alone at a lunch table.)

TAYLOR: *(To audience)* Reaction number two *(sits)*:

TAYLOR: *(Sighs)* Hey Jonah.

JONAH: Oh hey Tay, something wrong?

TAYLOR: You want the truth?

JONAH: Of course I want the truth.

TAYLOR: You won't judge?

JONAH: You are one of my best friends, Taylor. I would never judge you.

TAYLOR: Well you see, I've been having trouble with Dana lately, so I went up to see Ms. Hadley to see if she could help me work things out, but in the process I told her something very personal about myself and she wasn't very nice about it.

JONAH: What'd you tell her?

TAYLOR: Well, now I don't want to tell anyone else because I'm afraid they're going to act the same way.

JONAH: Ms. Hadley isn't everyone; other people may act differently and be nice about it. Just tell me what it is; maybe I can help.

TAYLOR: It's not really something that you can 'help.'

JONAH: Well, what is it?

TAYLOR: Jonah, I'm bi.

JONAH: Oh…really?

TAYLOR: Yeah…

TEACHER: Lunch is over kids, back to class!

(*TAYLOR and JONAH get up from the table and begin to walk to the edge of the stage.*)

JONAH: That's actually really cool, I've never had a friend that's bi before. And again, I would never judge you, I'll always love you anyway. There is absolutely nothing wrong with that.

TAYLOR: Thank you Jonah, that really means a lot to me.

(*TAYLOR and JONAH hug and JONAH exits the stage. TAYLOR walks back to the center.*)

TAYLOR: When I look back on it, I don't know why I even considered the first reaction as acceptable. Even if I was scared about it, it was who I was meant to be. Who was Ms. Hadley to go and tell me that I should change because she seemed to think that liking girls as well as guys wasn't 'natural'? I'm bi. It happens.

Harry Potter and the Network of Doom
by Dreams of Hope with Ted Hoover

CHARACTERS:

HARRY	RON	HERMIONE
STUDENTS		
REPORTER	TEACHER	ANCHOR

NOTE: *In the script names have been given to the ANCHOR, REPORTER, and TEACHER – Bob Brown, Sue Smith, and Mrs. White. However, the roles can be played by any gender and the character names should be the same as the ACTOR playing the part. Also, the students can be played by as many ACTORs as are available.*

SETTING: *We begin in darkness for a few beats. Then we hear the "Hedwig's Theme" cue from the movie. It fades as the lights come up. HARRY, HERMIONE and RON are Up Center in the middle of an intense conversation.*

HARRY: But Dumbledore said it's my destiny to fight Voldemort.

RON: That's right Hermione, he did.

HERMIONE: But Harry, Professor McGonagall told us not to leave the school grounds!

RON: That's right Harry, she did.

HERMIONE: They just want us to be safe!

HARRY: Then why stick us in a castle on a cliff over a lake with a three-headed dog?

RON: He's got a point, Hermione.

HERMIONE: But –

(They freeze and stay frozen. The ANCHOR enters Down Left.)

ANCHOR: We interrupt this broadcast of "Harry Potter and the Sippy Cup of Hot Soup" with a late breaking news bulletin. I'm Bob Brown. *(Looks to another "camera")* We're receiving reports that the local high school has exploded into chaos today when one of the students admitted… he's gay. We take you now to this scene of tragic turmoil with our reporter, Sue Smith. What's the situation like there Sue?

(The REPORTER is discovered Down Right.)

REPORTER: Thanks, Bob. It's like a war zone here! Tensions are running sky high and people who make things up for a living are saying that the riot police will be called in at any moment!

ANCHOR: We're getting unreliable reports that many of the students have collapsed in sheer terror.

REPORTER: According to unfounded gossip, several children had to be rushed to local hospitals from the shock.

(A group of STUDENTS enter Down Right, talking and laughing.)

REPORTER: Here's a few students, now. Let me see if any are conscious. *(to STUDENTS)* Pardon me! Sue Smith, Evening Action News. A gay student came out in your high school today. Your reaction?

STUDENT: Huh?

STUDENT: What?

REPORTER: People who don't know what they're talking about tell us that John Jones proclaimed during the middle of English class he is homosexual. Is it true that your screaming was so loud several lab rats exploded?

STUDENT: Screaming?

REPORTER: Did any of you faint?

STUDENT: She's talking about that short story John wrote.

STUDENT: Oh please, we've known John's been gay since, like, forever.

REPORTER: And yet you found the courage to eat lunch in the same room as him!

STUDENT: He's my locker partner.

REPORTER: *(Almost in tears)* You're so brave! What are your plans now?

STUDENT: I've got band practice.

REPORTER: No. What are your plans for getting John out of here? Should he be arrested? Shot out of a cannon? A giant slingshot maybe?

STUDENT: Why would we want to get rid of John? This is his school. He belongs here. *(They start to walk away.)*

STUDENT: You're weird. *(They exit)*

REPORTER: *(To camera)* As you can see Bob, these young people are so overwhelmed they don't even know how much pain they're in. Back to you. *(Exits)*

ANCHOR: Thanks, Sue. Stay tuned for more as this heartbreaking story develops. We return you to "Harry Potter and the Deathly Halitosis."
(ANCHOR exits as HARRY, HERMIONE, and RON unfreeze.)

HARRY: But I know Voldemort knows that I know that he knows that I know…that he knows. My scar's been hurting all day.

RON: It has, Hermione.

HERMIONE: Yeah, about that scar business. D'you ever think about maybe using a Band-Aid? I'm just saying, it might clear up.

RON: It could, Harry.

HARRY: I got it because my mother loved me.

RON: She did, Hermione.

HERMIONE: That's sweet and everything. But you're supposed to be the greatest wizard of your age, and you can't get rid of a little scar? Draco never shuts up about it.

RON: She's got a point, Harry.

HARRY: But –

RON: *(To HERMIONE)* You wanna get married?

(They freeze. ANCHOR returns.)

ANCHOR: We interrupt this broadcast of "Happy Potter and the Philosopher's Shopping List" to bring you an update on the shocking developments currently unfolding at the local high school. We go now to Sue Smith, our reporter at the scene. *(REPORTER is discovered Down Left with TEACHER.)* What is the mood like there, Sue?

REPORTER: A tornado of terror is tearing this school apart, Bob. I have here Mrs. White, the brave and gutsy teacher of the very English class where John Jones first began his campaign of panic.

TEACHER: I beg your pardon?

REPORTER: Mrs. White, can you describe this episode of agony?

TEACHER: What in the world are you talking about?

REPORTER: People who weren't there report shrieks of panic and torment echoing through the halls when John Jones revealed his secret life as a monster.

TEACHER: John read a short story he wrote about coming out to his family last year. It was very moving.

REPORTER: Is it true, Mrs. White, that the hair on several of the children's heads burst into flame?

TEACHER: Look, I thought you said you were doing a story on increased public school funding?

REPORTER: Do you need that extra money to build him a special cage?

TEACHER: What?

REPORTER: Uninformed web sites are claiming the police have yellow-taped the doors and windows and that John Jones is being flown to an island where he can't spread his gay germs.
TEACHER: *(Stern)* You need to stop this right now. John's one of my best students and one of the most popular kids in school.

REPORTER: Because he pretended to be one of them?

TEACHER: He IS one of them. Good afternoon.

(She exits.)

REPORTER: *(To camera)* As you can see Bob, the situation here is even worse than those badly spelled texts and Facebook comments have lead us to believe.

ANCHOR: Sue, I'm worried the teacher doesn't care that a stranger is inside that school!

REPORTER: Bob, I'm shocked how many of the students seemed to believe John Jones belongs there!

(HARRY, HERMINIONE, and RON slowly unfreeze, and, during the following, will slowly walk to Down Center, looking at ANCHOR and REPORTER in disbelief.)

ANCHOR: If children are exposed to difference and diversity at such a young age, can they ever be happy again?

REPORTER: According to people who don't know what they're talking about, John Jones has also managed to fool his own family, several friends, his pastor, and most of his neighbors into thinking he's a member of the community!

ANCHOR: Is this the end of civilization as we know it, Sue?

REPORTER: Not as long as you and I stay strong, Bob and report the news the way we want it to be!

ANCHOR: In this great struggle, Sue, we can't let them tell us who they are!

HARRY, HERMIONE & RON: Stupefy! *(ANCHOR and REPORTER freeze.)*

HARRY, HERMIONE & RON: *(After a beat they shrug their shoulders)* Muggles.

Kids in the Hall
by Ajenai Hampton

STUDENT A   STUDENT B   STUDENT C

Setting: School hallway.

STUDENT A: (*mocking the way B stands*) Hey guys, do I look gay yet?

STUDENT B: That's not funny, I'm just standing here.

STUDENT A: You're so gay, dude, it hurts my eyes just to look at you.

STUDENT B: What's that supposed to mean? I'm not even gay.

STUDENT A: Your best friend is gay, plus you're always wearing skinny jeans and tight clothes, and you talk totally gay.

STUDENT B: Just because my best friend is gay doesn't mean I'm gay too.

STUDENT A: Someone's in denial. (*kids snicker*) We'll help you out. We'll tell everyone in the school that you're gay, and that...

STUDENT C: (*interrupts*) What's going on here?

STUDENT A: N-nothing principal!

STUDENT C: B, are you being bullied?

STUDENT A: Of course he's not! We were just playing around!

STUDENT C: I wasn't asking you.

STUDENT B: No. We're fine

STUDENT A: Yeah, you heard him, we're fine.

STUDENT C: B, if anything is going on, come to my office and tell me.

STUDENT B: I will... don't worry.

(Principal walks away.)

STUDENT A: Dude you could have totally busted us for that, how come you didn't?

STUDENT B: I don't know. I think you're just bullying me because you can. I'm not gay and you know that, but maybe you have a bad home life. Or maybe you're the gay one here, and you're trying to hide it from your friends.

(Friends all laugh at A's embarrassment.)
STUDENT A: S-shut up! Get over here! *(drags B away to beat him up)*

STUDENT B: Stop!

STUDENT A: Listen...I...I actually am gay.

STUDENT B: You are?

STUDENT A: Yeah. I know I was mean to you. I'm sorry, but everyone would reject me if I told anyone.

STUDENT B: I won't tell anyone. Just stop being mean to me.

STUDENT A: I will. I just thought by calling other people gay, nobody would think I was gay.

STUDENT B: I understand, I won't out you if you don't feel ready, but just know you shouldn't hide yourself.

STUDENT A: Thanks, man.

STUDENT B: You're welcome.

Bully to the Brink

by Dreams of Hope with Vanessa German

I've done it.
Me too
Me too.
I laughed / giggled
CRACKED A JOKE AT SOMONE ELSE'S EXPENSE
I spread the rumor
made fun let it go on & on
& DIDN'T TRY TO STOP IT WHEN I WATCHED IT HAPPENING
TO SOMEONE ELSE
I-TURNED MY BACK
WHY?

Because I was with my friends
Because it made me feel good at the time /
I thought it was funny
I wanted to fit in
It made me feel
BIGGER STRONGER FASTER BADDER BETTER YOU BETTER
BELIEVE IT –

I'VE BEEN A BULLY TOO

ONE.

He did it for laughs
to pass the time
Said – it's no crime /
It's just THE WAY THINGS GO
Let them know you don't like
their hair
their clothes
their shoes
the way they walk
dance or move
or
WHO THEY CHOOSE TO BE WITH

see / if you are
MEAN ENOUGH & LOUD ENOUGH
/ people will just / FORGET EVERYTHING AND RUN

IN FEAR
& whoever can make the most people AFRAID – WINS
& it isn't my fault that you
Are an EASY TARGET / MORE BULLSEYE than HUMAN BEING /
BUT – you are
/ SO-READY AIM FIRE SHOOT & THE BANG IS A LAUGH
& I am
THE SHELL OF THE BULLET IN YOUR HEART /
With words
SHARP AS SHARDS
like a dagger to the gut /
I shoot
I stab
I cut
I laugh & just keep on
LAUGHING / STABBING / JABBING & POINTING – AT YOU
Because it's fun

Can't you take a joke?
Why are you crying?
Stand up /
Shut up /
YOU ARE SO FAKE
Forget everything and RUN /
it's just a Rumor /
Rumors can be true
rumors can be lies
take it with a grain of salt
STOP CRYING!

Remember
YOU'RE NOT A PERSON
YOU'RE A BULLSEYE
& your shoes are two sizes too small for my big feet
SO I AM GOING TO KEEP WALKING ALL OVER YOU

or maybe it's more complicated than that
maybe it's HOME
the fist
the punch
the fury
the kick
and the wooden spoon
maybe it's the

CHIP OF THE OLD BLOCK SYNDROME /
(put up your dukes)
my world I destroyed / so I become
A DESTROYER /
Why, because I can /
because my rage is my religion
my language
my way
& my reason for existing

WHY, BECAUSE
what I see in you
is what I despise
is what I so deeply tried to hide in
MYSELF

WHY, BECAUSE
I'M SCARED – SO I SCARE
I'M ASHAMED – SO I SHAME
I'M PAINED – SO I PAIN

EXPERTLY EXECUTING
THE   YOU   FROM   ME
SO NO ONE WILL SEE THE
MIRROR OF US
IN WE

now
I cannot stop looking at my hands
THESE HANDS
are blood red / with YOUR BLOOD
I shoved
MY SHOES – ON YOUR FEET
and never bothered to try on yours

WHY
because I aimed myself at you
READY
SHAME
FIRE
SHOOT
YOU – WERE MY ESCAPE
BECAUSE I KNOW I COULDN'T TAKE EVERYDAY – THE WAY –
YOU DD
TERRORIZED
VICTIMIZED
BRUTALIZED

NOW I CRY – BECAUSE I
TOOK IT OUT – ON YOU
& you took it out with a rope to the neck
a gun to the head
a razor to the wrist
pills to the mouth
a jump off the bridge

and now
I DON'T SLEEP WELL AT NIGHT
my mind runs rampant /
why   WHY   WHY

IF I COULD BRING YOU BACK TO LIFE I'D – JUST
STOP –
I'D WALK AWAY
I'D TRY WALKING THE HALLWAY IN THE MILE OF YOUR SHOES

IF I COULD BRING YOU BACK TO LIFE
I'D JUST SAY – I'M SORRY
I'D
mind my own business
let you be
I could have taken a moment to see that INSTEAD OF HATING OUR
DIFFERENCES
I COULD HAVE ACTUALLY – ADMIRED THEM
IF I HAD TAKEN THE TIME TO GET TO KNOW YOU MAYBE WE
COULD HAVE
BEEN

I DIDN'T THINK IT WOULD END THIS WAY
NO HAPPY ENDINGS EXCEPT TO SAY

I've done it.
Me too. Me too.
ME TOO
BUT NEXT TIME I'LL STOP TO THINK
WHAT HAPPENS (IF I) BULLY SOMEONE TO THE BRINK

More Than Enough
by Maya Brown

CHARACTERS:

TOM   HARRISON

SETTING: *HARRISON is sitting on a bench eating lunch. TOM walks across the stage, behind the bench and does a double take. HARRISON doesn't notice him. TOM walks back and sits down beside HARRISON. HARRISON notices but doesn't look up.*

TOM: Still a vegetarian I see.

HARRISON: *(Startled)* What the...? *(In recognition)* Dude! It's nice to see you.

TOM: You too! I haven't seen you in ages!

HARRISON: Yeah, not since school got out.

TOM: So how's your summer been? You still dating Cassie?

HARRISON: Nah, we broke up pretty soon after school ended.

TOM: Aw, I'm sorry.

HARRISON: It's fine, it was time. How about you? Any summer flings?

TOM: Well there is someone...

HARRISON: Yeah? Who? Do tell!

TOM: I've been talking to this guy I met at orientation, and I'm hoping we can like hang out once we get to college in the fall.

HARRISON: Nice, looks like you've got your first college romance all planned out already!

TOM: Hopefully!

HARRISON: Well what's his name? Is he cute?

TOM: His name's Jake, and yeah, he's got a little bit of the surfer look going on, but he's super cute, and he's really into music just like me.

HARRISON: That's awesome. You can write him some sappy indie love songs or something.

TOM: Yeah totally, guys eat that right up.

HARRISON: Haha yeah. So Tom...

TOM: What?

HARRISON: Well this is kind of awkward, but I always meant to tell you, all that crap that went down last year. You know, when those guys were being mean to you and basically making you quit football and stuff...

TOM: Yeah.

HARRISON: Well, that was, like, really awful of them. And I'm really sorry that happened. It shouldn't have. They were jerks... *(Pause)* I dunno, my cousin just came out and she's having a rough time of it and I just felt bad that I never really did anything to help you out, and I wanted you to know that me and a lot of the guys were like gonna step in if any of them said anything ever again.

TOM: Thanks man. It was a rough year, but I always knew I had you guys to back me up or to vent to and that helped a lot.

HARRISON: Yeah, I just wish I could've done more you know? Those guys got off way too easy.

TOM: Too bad we don't live in the 1950s, we could've staged a rumble.

HARRISON: *(Chuckles)* No but seriously, Coach Mathews didn't even do anything. The guys and I were really mad about that, we almost went to the principal over it.

TOM: Wow. I never knew that.

HARRISON: Well, we didn't want to like make it a bigger deal for you than it already was. We figured it was hard enough without us pushing it, and you seemed happy to just quit and let it blow over.

TOM: Yeah, I was pretty much done with football by that point. I wasn't destined for the NFL or anything.

HARRISON: I get it, we can't all be the star quarterback can we?

TOM: *(Laughs)* Ok, let's stop talking football, I'm so over it.

HARRISON: Sure, sure. I guess a part of me wishes I had gone to the principal. I felt like kind of a terrible friend just letting it go.

TOM: Nah man, you made sure I knew you were there for me, and that's all I really needed.

HARRISON: Ok, sorry for bringing it up again, it's just been nagging at me recently.

TOM: No problem.

HARRISON: Oh, I meant to ask you, are you going to the Pride Festival next week? My cousin wants someone to go with her, so I was thinking of driving her down.

TOM: Yeah, me and a few of my friends from the Gay Straight Trans Alliance are gonna make a day of it. Want to come with us?

HARRISON: That'd be great, I mean, as fun as cousin bonding time sounds, I'd rather have a few other people around.

TOM: No problem, it'll be fun to have you there. We'll get you some rainbow swag for your dorm room.

HARRISON: No thanks, I don't want to ward off the girls.

TOM: Oh please, girls love guys who love gays.

HARRISON: *(Laughs)* Sure....

TOM: Ok, I've gotta go, my lunch break is ridiculously short.

HARRISON: Alright. It was nice running into you man.

TOM: You too.

HARRISON: Bye! *(Turns to leave)*

TOM: Oh and Harrison?

HARRISON: Yeah bud?

TOM: What you were saying before? About stepping in last year?

HARRISON: Yeah?

TOM: You've done more than enough.

History of "Gay"
by Maeve Porter Holliday

According to a guy at school today, I am the "definition of gay."
According to Dictionary.com, as a man in the 1800's, I had or showed
a merry, lively mood.

Synonyms: Cheerful, gleeful, happy, glad, cheery, light-hearted,
joyous, joyful, jovial; sunny, lively, vivacious, sparkling; chipper,
playful, jaunty, sprightly, blithe.

Antonyms: Serious, grave, solemn, joyless; staid, sedate; unhappy,
morose, grim; sad, depressed, melancholy.

As a man in the 1900's, I am bright or showy: gay colors; gay
ornaments.

Synonyms: Colorful, brilliant, vivid, intense, lustrous; glittering,
theatrical, flamboyant.

Antonyms: Dull, drab, somber, lackluster; conservative.

Today, I am a "Slang: Often Disparaging and Offensive. Awkward,
stupid, or bad; lame." I have become an insult rather than a merry
man. I have become the opposite of what I am. So no, I am not the
definition of "gay" today. I am not stupid or offensive or lame. I am
a smart, chipper, playful, vivacious, jovial, theatrical man, who loves
another man.

Pride Grow Advertisement
by Dreams of Hope with Ted Hoover

CHARACTERS:

BOSS	ROBIN WORTH, a new worker
QUESTIONER	CO-WORKERS
3 SATISFIED CUSTOMERS	NARRATOR

SETTING: *Workplace. Opens with BOSS leading ROBIN around and introducing ROBIN to other staff.*

BOSS: Hello, everyone, I would like you to meet Robin Worth. Robin, these are your
Fellow co-workers here at Schmoogle.com

(ROBIN puts hand out to shake hands with QUESTIONER.)

QUESTIONER: Are you gay?

(ROBIN looks shocked and horrified. All freeze.)

NARRATOR: Has this ever happened to you? Is your sexuality frequently in question? Do you feel like disappearing into a wall or like hitting someone? Then you need Pride Grow. Listen to some of our satisfied customers.

CUSTOMER 1: Before Pride Grow, I was locked in the closet of self-hate. I couldn't write a rhyme. But, with Pride Grow, I'm the gay Ludacris.

(Freeze and pause.)

CUSTOMER 2: Before Pride Grow I would never take my mother's calls because I didn't want to talk about my sexuality. Now, with Pride Grow, I call her!

(*Freeze and pause. All three CUSTOMERS break into song.*)

Pride Grow Jingle
(swing feel)

C   C   D D E
When you're feeling glum

C   C D   D   E   E   F
And you don't know what to do,

G G   G   C
Buy some Pride Grow

D E   D C
It's good for you

(*Re-do scene with new ending.*)

QUESTIONER: "Are you gay?"

ROBIN: Yes, I am!

ALL: (*With cheerleader arms*) Yay! (*Thumbs up to audience*) Buy Pride Grow!

It Gets Better
by Kaitlin Hunter, arr. by Douglas Levine for Dreams of Hope

I know you feel like no one cares,
Stuck in a bottomless pit of despair.
Reaching your hand up to the sky, tryin' to find something to hold.
I'm here to tell you if can survive the cold,

Chorus
It gets better…
You can depend on me whenever you need a friend.
It gets better…
I know for sure that the sun will shine again.
It gets better…
Even when you feel alone, you're never really on your own.
It gets better, gets better,
If you feel me, sing along.

Don't let those haters drag you down.
Cast off that burden before you drown.
I know you're lonely, but don't believe you're the only one
To wanna surrender before the fight's even begun!

Chorus

You are loved and you matter.
Your dreams no one can shatter.
It can all change in a blink,
'Cause you're stronger than you think…thank you think.

Chorus 2x
If you feel me, sing along.
If you feel me, sing along.

It Gets Better

Words and Music by Kaity Hunter
Arr. Douglas Levine

2

It Gets Better

Letters
by Dreams of Hope with Ted Hoover

CHARACTERS:

SHANAI   EVAN   BEN

SHANAI: If I could write a letter to my twelve-year-old self, there are a lot of things I would tell her.

EVAN: Dear me, I know that right now you don't trust anyone, anything.

BEN: Dear Struggling, I remember when I was in your shoes: terrified to tell the truth,
 afraid that no one would understand.

SHANAI: I would tell her that you are beautiful no matter what people may tell you.

BEN: Fearful of their words, and scared of being gay. I was beaten up, made fun of, kept
on the outside, nearly bullied to the brink, and I thought that I had lost myself   completely.

EVAN: All the lies they told you are racing / through your heart / through our mind /
we've trapped everything they said to us / inside.

SHANAI: If I could write a letter to my twelve year-old self, I'd tell her that your crush on little Sarah is not something to be frightened about or try to fix.

EVAN: We've been / Broken and Beaten / Abandoned and Abused / Waiting for the
World to end.

BEN: But I was also angry at myself for my fear and cowardice.

EVAN: Trembling / With words unverbalized / Shivering / a shallow breath we breathe /
and whisper good night / Is all we could do.

SHANAI: If I could write a letter for my twelve year-old self, I'd tell her to not fear
judgment or unkindness, not everyone will like you, but everyone should respect you.

BEN: I know that you're struggling, and I know how it feels to have people make you feel worthless, with all the pain held in your heart,

SHANAI: I would tell her that many people will enter and leave your life for a variety
of reasons; if they are good, enjoy and nurture their time with you, if they aren't, let them go as soon as possible.

BEN: But raise yourself up. It's okay to be scared, but you are just as normal, deserving, and meaningful as anyone else.

EVAN: Dear me / you brave and stubborn / pure in your innocence,

BEN: All you have to do is stay strong.

SHANAI: I would tell her that you are a lot more amazing than you think.

EVAN: I want you to read this letter,

BEN: And when it seems like your hope is gone, just move along.

SHANAI: Because of everything else you have to offer. A lot of people will see it.

EVAN: Hear my plea / unselfishly / trust your heart and know / It does get better.

BEN: Just remember that it will get better.

SHANAI: Hang in there and continue to blossom into the woman you will become.

Letter to a Young One
words by AllyKay Kamlet and Douglas Levine,
music by Douglas Levine for Dreams of Hope

INTRO
Ooh. Ooh. Ooh.

Verse I
Dear young one,
Since I was you, so much has changed.
All the confusion and pain have been rearranged
Into a life I live without regret.
I have the job they said I'd never get.
I have the love they thought would never last,
And the strength that comes from surviving your past.

Pre-chorus I
If I could cradle your face in my hands,
I'd look deep into those shining eyes of yours, and say:

Chorus I
Don't give up on your dreams.
And trust me, I know it's as tough as it seems.
But with all your courage and poise,
If you can block out the noise,
Then I guarantee it gets better.

Interlude
Ooh. Ooh. Ooh.

Verse II
Oh, young one,
When I was you, I'd lay in bed,
Letting the things that they said to me fill my head.
And there were times I thought, "I can't go on.
Why should each day feel like a marathon?
When will they get a life and let me be,
So I can smile, again, and just be me?"

Pre-chorus II
I know you think that your options are few,
But, I'm telling you now: there's so much in store for you!
Chorus 2x

Outro 4x
GROUP 1: Ooh. Ooh. Ooh…Who.
SOLO or GROUP 2: Dear young one.

Letter To A Young One

Words by Ally Kay & Douglas Levine
Music by Douglas Levine

Letter To A Young One

4 feel

mp

Letter To A Young One

Letter To A Young One

AIDS Report
by Gabrielle Maalihan

CHARACTERS:

CINDY   TEACHER
HENRY   KEVIN

CINDY: Then, in June 20, 1848, the Seneca Falls conference ended. And that's my report. Oh, wait! It ended in July. That's the end of my report. Thank you. Oh, I would also like to add that--

TEACHER: Thank you Cindy, your essay on the triangle-shirt-waist-factory was... very factually accurate. Henry, are you ready to present?

HENRY: Yes.

TEACHER: Well go ahead then.

HENRY: I did my essay on the AIDS epidemic.

CINDY: That wasn't on the list of suggested topics.

KEVIN: Shut up, Cindy.

TEACHER: Language! And no talking. But, she is right, Henry. That was not the list of suggested topics.

HENRY: Yes, I know. But it should have been.

TEACHER: The assignment was to write about one of the major tragedies of the 20th century. Now, if you can't abide by the criteria, I'll have no choice but to give you an F. Ali, don't sleep in my class!

KEVIN: Don't you think that's a little harsh?

TEACHER: Sass me one more time. Henry, what do you say to this? Either you follow the criteria or fail.

HENRY: I did follow the criteria. I wrote my essay about the topic, and it is five pages long, with no grammatical errors.

TEACHER: Henry, that is not the point! This AIDS topic you chose is not relevant enough, nor is it tragic enough for-

HENRY: AIDS was officially recognized in 1981. By then, 159 people reportedly died of AIDS. The epidemic was spreading rapidly through the queer community.

TEACHER: Stop it this instant. This subject is not appropriate for-

HENRY: A year later, the death rate had risen by 618. In 1983, 2,118 deaths...

TEACHER: Sit down now! Henry, I'm going to call your mother. Cindy, sit down.

HENRY: Then 5,596, 12,529, 24,559, 40,849, and by 1988, there were 61,816 recorded deaths. But the signs of the epidemic started even longer before.

TEACHER: I will not have this talk about a bunch of faggots in my classroom!

CINDY: You can't say that!

HENRY: By1976, San Francisco had fallen to the epidemic. As it grew, up to 50% of the population was infected and the San Franciscan community was devastated.

KEVIN: Let him speak.

HENRY: *(stops reading paper)* Too many died. Every week, the newspaper was filled with obituaries. Communities were being destroyed and no one even seemed to notice. No one wanted to deal with the "gay disease." But I couldn't put that in my paper, because there isn't even any research on it. None. We've never heard about it on TV, or read it in a history book. It's not on your list of suggested topics. But it happened. My uncle died of AIDS in 1978. He was 20 when he died. And no one in my family, no one talks about it, because they're ashamed about how and what he died from. I could tell you I know the exact numbers of all the people who died of AIDS. But that would be a lie. Because I don't know, no one knows, and that is a tragedy.

Why It Matters
by Maeve Porter Holliday

CHARACTERS:
MOMMY
MAMA
GIRL: MOMMY and MAMA's 11 year-old daughter

SETTING: *Dim lights up on stage. MOMMY and MAMA sit in chairs facing each other. GIRL stands in the corner of the stage. Voices on the radio quietly discuss the results of the recent vote: the right to same-sex marriage is denied. GIRL exits, quietly sobbing. Lights focus on MOMMY and MAMA. MOMMY stares off into the audience while MAMA has her head in her hands.*

MOMMY: *(Speaking to MAMA)* She won't understand why we have to postpone the wedding. She's only eleven, she'll think that the state doesn't accept the way we live and who we love. *(Pauses)* How can we tell her that our church, our home, does not want us to be able to get married?

MAMA: It is more than that! They basically said that we did not deserve the ones we love. *(After fuming, calms down and holds MOMMY's hand)* I don't want to have to go to another state to marry the woman I love. I want *you*, I want our home, I want our child to understand that we will win our equality next time.

(Lights dim, scene shifts to a small bedroom, GIRL is on the floor clutching her knees in towards her chest. MOMMY and MAMA enter together and join her on the ground, mimicking her motions. MOMMY and MAMA are at a loss for words.)

GIRL: They said no. *(Pauses, waiting for an answer)* Maine said no? Mama, can you not love Mommy anymore? Will I stay with you? Will you stay together? *(GIRL's face falls as she begins to sob. MAMA and MOMMY look stunned)*

MAMA: *(Fiercely and lovingly)* You will always be our baby girl. You will always stay with us. We will always love you. They cannot separate us. *(Pauses)* All they said was that we have to wait to be officially married here.

MOMMY: *(Grips MAMA's hand. Turns GIRL towards her with tears streaming down her face)* Baby, of course we will stay together. Labels don't change anything, we still love each other. This is not a no; this is a not yet. We will keep fighting for our marriage. It is them that we should pity because they don't have such a beautiful girl in their lives, such a beautiful partner, and a beautiful life. Nothing will change. We will still be a family.

GIRL: *(Stands up and faces audience)* What does it mean when some people have rights over others? When some can marry who they love, and others are scorned for loving. Why is it that some people can care for their partners by being in the hospital room, while others are banned? My Mommy had breast cancer and Mama could not visit her without a marriage license and all of the paperwork. Another woman in the same room had her husband come into the room by showing the staff the wedding ring. *(Walking over to MAMA, GIRL crouches by her side)* Mama, will you still love Mommy if you cannot get married? Will a piece of paper change anything?

MAMA: I will love your mother no matter what gets in our way, and I want to make our love legal by paper, but paper makes a whole lot of difference. Do you remember when Mommy fell down the stairs and broke her leg? I could not even sign the paper to allow them to operate. *(Looks at MOMMY)* What if something major had happened and she died because I could not give them permission to save her?

(Scene switches to a church as GIRL speaks.)

GIRL: *(Towards the audience, to herself.)* If I had a "normal" family with one mom and one dad, would I be loved differently? Or is it the same love between a parent and a child no matter the sexuality or sexual orientation? How is my moms' love any different from the love between my dad and his wife? Why does it matter who loves who if love is the ultimate motive? My Mommy loved my dad at one point, but their love for each other faded. They make each other unhappy. Why can't love just be happiness? Being gay is not evil or different; being gay is to love a person who is the same sex as yourself. My mothers love each other. *(MOMMY and MAMA walk up behind GIRL, holding hands)* But under God or State people think of their love as "wrong." It is just love. I want my moms to get married. I want my family to stay together and have the same rights and recognitions.

Rainbow Cupcakes
by Maya Brown, Treva deMaynadier, and Mollie Pleau

CHARACTERS:

GIRL 1 LEVEL 1	LEVEL 3	LEVEL 5
GIRL 2 LEVEL 2	LEVEL 4	LEVEL 6

SETTING: *GIRL 1 and GIRL 2, who have been best friends since kindergarten, are out for coffee after school. GIRL 1 decides she wants to come out to GIRL 2 as gay.*

GIRL 1: Can you believe we have to make cupcakes for French class tomorrow? I have so much homework! I don't want to have to worry about cupcakes too...

GIRL 2: I know, right?

GIRL 1: Let's get some coffee now. School was brutal today.

GIRL 2: You're telling me.

GIRL 1: Oh my god. I have *news* for you.

GIRL 2: What? Tell me! What?

GIRL 1: Well, you know my cousin right?

GIRL 2: Wait, which one?

GIRL 1: Janie. *Anyway*. She just got engaged.

GIRL 2: Who's the lucky man?

GIRL 1: Well... it's not actually a man. It's a girl.

GIRL 2: Oh... that's cool...

(*GIRL 1 and GIRL 2 pause awkwardly.*)

GIRL 1: I've actually wanted to tell you something for a while...

GIRL 2: What? You don't have to be so dramatic. Just tell me.

GIRL 1: I'm gay.

(*GIRL 1 and GIRL 2 freeze. LEVELS 1-6 enter one by one and stand in a line behind them and come forward. Each LEVEL storms out after their line. Play with dramatic storming depending on number of people.*)

LEVEL 1: Uh yeah, everyone already knows that already. People talk about it all of the time.

LEVEL 2: I always knew our friendship was too close. You've always had a crush on me, haven't you?

LEVEL 3: My mom won't let you come over anymore. There's no way she'd understand.

LEVEL 4: Why would you choose this for yourself? You've never even had sex with a guy. How would you know?

LEVEL 5: I hope you know you're going to hell!

LEVEL 6: I can't be seen with you anymore. You disgust me. We can't be friends.

(*GIRL 1 and GIRL 2 unfreeze.*)

GIRL 2: I'm so glad you told me. I hope you didn't worry too much about it.

GIRL 1: So do you want to get going now so we can make those cupcakes?

GIRL 2: We can even make them rainbow!

Independence Day
by Dreams of Hope

CHARACTERS:

FATHER	GRANDMOTHER	GRANDFATHER
BROTHER	GIRLFRIEND	GAY DAUGHTER
UNCLE	COUSIN	AUNT

SETTING: *Backyard picnic. Table or bench set up, lawn chairs, and a small outside grill.*

(FATHER and GRANDFATHER are standing around the grill. FATHER is cooking, while GRANDFATHER is watching closely. GRANDMOTHER is sitting peacefully in one of the lawn chairs.)

GRANDFATHER: Don't burn them now.

FATHER: I won't, Dad.

GRANDFATHER: You couldn't if you tried; that's a wimpy fire.

FATHER: They'll be fine, Dad.

GRANDMOTHER: Are we at the zoo, Clark?

FATHER: No, Ma, you're at our house for the 4th of July... and my name's not Clark.

GRANDMOTHER: What did you say Clark?

GRANDFATHER: *(Loudly)* He said his name isn't Clark, you old goat!

GRANDMOTHER: That's nice, Clark.

(GRANDFATHER just shrugs towards FATHER.)

MOTHER: *(Rushing on stage)* Alright, our in-laws are going to be here any minute. Oh,
and Liz doesn't want you to embarrass her in front of her new friend.

FATHER: She always has a new friend. Where does she get all these new friends?

GRANDFATHER: What's wrong with having a few friends?

MOTHER: Oh nothing, it's just that they always seem to be very close and…

BROTHER: *(Entering)* Get ready, they're here.

(AUNT, COUSIN, and UNCLE enter. UNCLE lags behind and joins the group around the grill; COUSIN starts to talk with BROTHER; AUNT rushes to the table and places a huge bowl on the table.)

AUNT: *(With an annoying melody)* Hello Hellooooooo! I brought the potato salad!

MOTHER: *(Pretending to be excited)* Hello! How was the ride?

AUNT: Fine, fine. *(To BROTHER)* Come give your aunt a hug. *(Grabs BROTHER and gives him a big exaggerated hug, then pinches his cheek)* Would you look at his face, how adorable. Now, where's the other one?

MOTHER: Oh, she went to get her friend who's joining us. She wants everyone to meet
her and wants to tell us something.

AUNT: Oh, I love surprises.

GRANDMOTHER: Who's birthday is it, Clark?

GRANDFATHER: It's no one's birthday, it's the 4th of July!

(GAY DAUGHTER and GIRLFRIEND enter.)

AUNT: Hellooooo!

GRANDMOTHER: Happy Birthday!

GRANDFATHER: It's a 4th of July party!

GAY DAUGHTER: Hey everyone, we just came by to say hello, and head back out.

MOTHER: Head back out? You just arrived.

GAY DAUGHTER: Well, we both decided that we shouldn't celebrate the 4th of July.

FATHER: Why not? The whole family is here.

UNCLE: Plus, we celebrate our independence.

GAY DAUGHTER: Well, not everyone gets the full rights that they deserve.

BROTHER: What are you talking about?

COUSIN: Yeah, this is the land of the free.

AUNT: (*Noticing the tension building*) Would you look at that table setting, how cute!

UNCLE: Who doesn't get full rights?

GAY DAUGHTER: Gays, Lesbians, Bisexuals, and Transgender people.

AUNT: When do the fireworks start? I love watching fireworks.

FATHER: That's because they don't deserve rights.

GIRLFRIEND: What?

MOTHER: You don't have to worry about that because you aren't any of those, isn't that
right dear?

COUSIN: Do we really want to find out?

AUNT: Who wants some potato salad, huh? Mmmmm, doesn't it look good.

GAY DAUGHTER: Mom, Dad, everybody...I'm bisexual.

FATHER, UNCLE, GRANDFATHER: What?!

BROTHER: You're bisexual? That's pretty hot... wait, you're my sister!

MOTHER: I think I need to sit down. (*Falls back into a chair*)

GRANDMOTHER: (*Notices MOTHER who has fallen in the chair next to hers*)
Oh, hello dear, nice party isn't it? When do we sing happy birthday?

AUNT: Perhaps this isn't the best time to do this.

GAY DAUGHTER: I might as well get it over with.

FATHER: I did not raise any bisexual.

GRANDFATHER: I did not raise any father to raise any bisexual.

BROTHER: So wait, you like girls and guys?

MOTHER: That's enough.

GRANDFATHER: You're letting the food burn.

GAY DAUGHTER: There's more.

COUSIN: You mean, there's more?

UNCLE: It's not like you have a girlfriend or anything.

GAY DAUGHTER: Her name is April.

GIRLFRIEND: Hey. (*Waves*)

(*Everyone except GAY DAUGHTER and GIRLFRIEND fall back into a chair. GRANDMOTHER starts to sing "Happy Birthday." MOTHER stops her half way.*)

MOTHER: No mom, we just heard about our daughter's friend.

GRANDMOTHER: Oh, that's nice.

BROTHER: No, grandma, she swings both ways.

GRANDMOTHER: What do you mean?

UNCLE: She's interested in members of the same and opposite sex.

GRANDMOTHER: I still don't understand.

AUNT: (*Loudly*) For heaven's sake! She likes both men and women! She's a bisexual!

GRANDMOTHER: Is that it? So am I.

EVERYONE BUT GRANDMOTHER: What?!

GRANDMOTHER: I was quite the looker back then, and I got the eye from both guys
and gals. I even had a few girlfriends, but I fell in love with your grandfather, he was the guy for me, so I married him. We all fall in love with someone, even if they're a girl or a boy. Just don't tell your grandfather, it'll be our secret.

GRANDFATHER: I'm right here, you unpredictable dinosaur.

GRANDMOTHER: Who are you?

AUNT: Well, this has been one crazy day, hasn't it? Why don't we all get something to
eat and maybe we can talk about it some more after we have settled down a bit?

GRANDFATHER: Chef Boyardee over here burned all the food.

AUNT: I hope everyone likes potato salad!

"Love many things,
for therein lies the true strength,
and whosoever loves much performs much,
and can accomplish much,
and what is done in love is done well."
- *Vincent Van Gogh*

Love

When I Was Little
by Sam Doughty

When I was little, I remember asking my mom a question. I asked her if guys kissed and stuff too. My mom replied to me, "That's not appropriate to talk about." So, I asked my grandmother, and she goes to church, so she said, "Homosexuality is witchcraft." But I didn't get it. I couldn't quite picture Harry Potter dating a guy. So, I asked my grandfather. He replied, "That's a question for when you're older."

So I got confused, and I came to the conclusion that when I'm older, I'm going to go to an inappropriate school called Hogwarts, where people will all be gay and evil. So I told my mom, and she laughed, and told me to go play outside. That's a true story. I asked because I saw a movie with guys kissing, not because I daydream.

First Love
by Kaitlin Hunter, arr. by Douglas Levine for Dreams of Hope

Verse I
I remember when I first saw your face
It was so beautiful in all its shining grace
I couldn't believe when you talked to me
I swear I couldn't breathe
But the look in your eye put me at ease
I was high above the clouds
All I could hear was my heart beating oh so loud.

Chorus
I felt so blessed the day that I found you
You got me doing things I thought that I'd never do
This is something that I've never felt before
All I know is that I want more.

Verse II
Love is something that I never thought I'd find
In fact it never crossed my mind
The more I talked to you, and knew you it was clear you were the one
Who could love me and I could love too
You are my first true love
I'm convinced you were sent from up above.

First Love

Words and Music by
Kaitlin Hunter
Arr. D. Levine

First Love

First Love

3

I'm con - vinced_____ that you were sent from a - bove._____ I felt

(2ndX vocal ad-lib)

oh so blessed the day that I found you. You got me do - in' things I thought that I'd

nev - er do._ This is some - thing that I've nev - er felt be - fore. All_ I

know is that I want_ more._____ I felt

more,_____ and more._____

more._____

Crush
by Sam Doughty

CHARACTERS:

ZACK	LANA	TEACHER 1
CRISSY	MRS. JONES	TEACHER 2
JACK		

SCENE I

SETTING: *After school in the park.*

ZACK: So, um, do you have any plans for this summer?

CRISSY: I don't really know yet. Do you?

ZACK: Well, I thought I would just hang out with friends.

CRISSY: Oh, that's cool. I probably will too. Not many other choices.

ZACK: *(Laughs softly)* Yeah, I know. Well, um, maybe we could spend some time together.

(ZACK and CRISSY pause awkwardly for three seconds.)

CRISSY: Well, I guess we could hang out or something.

ZACK: Yeah, that would be nice.

CRISSY: I um, have to go, my mom wants me home before four o'clock.

ZACK: Okay. Um, see you at school tomorrow.

CRISSY: Kay, bye.

SCENE II

SETTING: *School, first period.*

TEACHER 1: As you all know, I assigned you a writing prompt last night. If you finished, please hand it in.

ZACK: *(Whispers)* Hey Jack! Guess what?

JACK: *(Whispers)* What is it this time?

ZACK: I have decided to ask out Crissy!

JACK: What? Since when?

ZACK: Since last night.

TEACHER: *(Interrupts ZACK and JACK)* Excuse me gentlemen, is there something you
would like to share with the class?

ZACK: Nope. Afraid not.

TEACHER 1: Then I'll have to ask that you be quiet.

ZACK: Yeah, whatever.

TEACHER 1: I have an assignment for all of you. I want an essay on why you think this class is important. It is due on Friday. *(Class sighs)* Class is dismissed. *(Bell rings.)*

SCENE III

SETTING: *School, second period - science class.*

TEACHER 2: All right class, today we will be measuring the volume, density, and mass of objects. You will be assigned partners.

ZACK: Hey, Crissy, do you want to be lab partners?

CRISSY: Um, I don't think we can choose.

ZACK: Just answer.

CRISSY: *(Sighs)* Sure, but you have to pay attention, okay?

ZACK: I promise.

TEACHER 2: I hope you like your partners because they will be permanent for the last three and a half weeks of school.

CRISSY: You'd better actually work, Zack.

ZACK: I will Crissy. I want to ask you something. Um… *(Sighs)* I wanted to know if you… um...

CRISSY: What is it?

ZACK: Are you busy Friday night?

CRISSY: I can't. I'm sorry Zack, but I'm already dating someone.

ZACK: Who?

CRISSY: Zack, I'm bisexual. I'm dating a girl from a different town. Her name is
Chandler.

ZACK: Oh.

CRISSY: I knew that you would reject me if I told you!

ZACK: I'm not rejecting you; I'm just trying to process what you just said.

CRISSY: Well, it seems a lot like it. I'm sorry I didn't tell you. I was just afraid you might react the wrong way!

TEACHER 2: Is everything okay?

CRISSY: Fine.

ZACK: Fine!

SCENE IV

SETTING: *Lunch in the cafeteria.*

LANA: Hey Crissy, why do you look so bummed?

CRISSY: Because, in third period today, Zack… he asked me out.

LANA: Oh, that clears the picture. Did you have to tell him?

CRISSY: Yeah, I did. And I think he took it the wrong way. He seems really depressed.

LANA: Oh, that sucks.

CRISSY: Yeah, I don't know if he will be my friend. He seems to be avoiding me.

LANA: It's most likely just a guy thing; I doubt it has anything to do with your sexuality.

CRISSY: Maybe, I just hope we can still be friends. I don't want anything to come between us.

LANA: I know what you mean; you two have been friends for like, ever.

CRISSY: Exactly. I'll try to talk to him. Thanks for the help Lana. You're a great friend.

LANA: Anytime!

SCENE V

SETTING: *After school at ZACK's house.*

ZACK: Crissy, dating a girl? I would never have seen it coming. When I think about her, all I see is that caring smile she always gave when we talked. I can't give up. I won't. I can succeed. Think on the bright side: what bright side? Well, she's bi so I might have a chance someday. I can't change what's happened, it's just not possible. I guess I must just be depressed. Honestly, I don't even know. It sounds pathetic doesn't it?

(Knocking on front door.)

CRISSY: Zack, it's me, Crissy.

MRS. JONES: *(Answers door)* Hello Crissy, you must be looking for Zack. Come on in.

CRISSY: Thank you.

MRS. JONES: Zack! Crissy is here; she wants to talk to you!

ZACK: I'll be right down Mom!

MRS. JONES: Can I get you something to drink Crissy?

CRISSY: No thank you Mrs. Jones. I'm not thirsty.

MRS. JONES: Well, I'll be out gardening if you need me.

CRISSY: Okay, thank you.

ZACK: *(Enters room)* Um, hi.

CRISSY: Hi, I um, wanted to apologize for not telling you.

ZACK: Oh, it's fine. I overreacted anyway.

CRISSY: So, are we still friends?

ZACK: Yeah, friends.

Talking in my Sleep
by Megan E. Tripaldi

I talk in my sleep. It's an unusual way to start a conversation, but it's
something you need to know right off the bat. I've always done it,
ever since I was a kid. I have been known to say things like, "there
are tiny cameras everywhere," or wake myself up in mid conversation with someone I meet in my dreams. I never talk about what
I'm dreaming about, and what I say has never been relevant to my
thoughts…except once.

I was fourteen years-old, and I was at sleep-away camp. It was an
all-girls camp, tucked away in the New Hampshire mountains. We
were on an overnight camping trip and my friends and I had claimed
a spot on a hill in the woods to sleep. We did the usual: stay up as late
as we could, talking until we'd nod off one by one. Sadly, I was one of
the first few to go. Very early the next morning when I woke up one
of my friends told me something quite shocking… I'd confessed my
feelings to one of the girls in my sleep.
Apparently I said to the girl I was crushing on, "I like you as more
than a friend."

I was horrified. Not only did I admit my feelings to a straight girl in
my sleep, but I had just come to terms with liking girls not a month or
so before. I asked her if the girl knew, and, being the great friend she
was, she lied. "No, uh…she was asleep. Yeah, I'm pretty sure she was
asleep. She doesn't know. It's fine." It wasn't fine, and she knew. She
was awake for the whole thing. The rest of the term was miserable
for me. She avoided me. Names flew at me like bricks. I was beyond
mortified. People told me not to "have my lesbian feelings" around
them. I was called disgusting, sinner, dyke. I wanted to hide and cry
every time somebody looked at me. The worst part was I hadn't even
done anything consciously. What would have happened if I had?

Finally, the last day of camp came. Most of the horrible things people were saying had died down and I had moved on. Yet she came up to me, smiling with tears in her eyes and hugged me. "I'm sorry," she said. Bewildered by what was happening, all I could get out was, "Me too," even though I had nothing to apologize for, and we both knew it. I was overwhelmed with the "end of camp sadness" that everybody gets, so I smiled and let it go, but I was hurt for a very long time. Needless to say I haven't seen her since, but I have thought about that time often, even if I never talk about it. It was a turning point in my life; I couldn't deny my feelings anymore. If I did, they would come out anyway, so why fight it?

As far as the sleep-talking goes, I have never said anything like that since.

The Two Princes
by Ajenai Hampton

CHARACTERS:

NARRATOR	KING	QUEEN
PRINCE	LIBRAIAN	PRINCE 2

NARRATOR: Once upon a time, in a kingdom far, far away, there lived a young prince.

PRINCE: He lived in the castle with the-

KING: King-

QUEEN: -and Queen-

PRINCE: -Of the kingdom.

NARRATOR: But the king and queen weren't his real parents, they were his aunt and his uncle.

PRINCE: And my aunt and uncle took over as rulers of the kingdom.

KING: Now that we have our own baby boy, he can be ruler of the kingdom!

QUEEN: But honey, our nephew is still the proper heir of the throne. With his mother and father dead, he is next in line after us, not our son."

KING: Then we shall kill the prince! Once he is dead nothing shall stop our boy from becoming king!

NARRATOR: One night, the prince was woken up early in the morning by the kingdom librarian."

LIBRARIAN: Young highness…? Young highness! (*Shakes PRINCE*)

PRINCE: Wha…huh? What, I'm up, I'm up! …wait a second…what time is it?

LIBRARIAN: Your aunt and uncle have just given birth to a baby boy.

PRINCE: Really? Good for them, now let me sleep.

LIBRARIAN: No! You must run! The king will have his men kill you if you stay, so that the king's son can inherit the throne next!

PRINCE: What? Aw, man, not cool. (*He gets out of bed and runs away.*)

KING: Knights! The prince will not escape us! Find him! Bring him back and lock him in the dungeon!

(*The knights catch him, as they place in him in the dungeon.*)

PRINCE: You won't get away with this! I will escape this dungeon and when I do, then the throne will be mine – as it rightfully is!

NARRATOR: Several months later-

PRINCE 2: -A prince from another kingdom rescued the prince from the dungeon.

PRINCE: Help! Oh, help I say!

PRINCE 2: Hark! What is this I hear? The desperate cries of a soul in need? Who's there?

PRINCE: Me! I am the prince of this castle but my wicked aunt and uncle stole the throne from me! I want it back!

PRINCE 2: Fear not. I shall rescue you!

(*They escape and run away from the kingdom.*)

PRINCE: Thank you! Will you help me free my kingdom?

PRINCE 2: Of course I will! By the way I'm Tom.

PRINCE: Good to meet ya. Xavier

NARRATOR: They stormed the castle using the army from the other kingdom and captured his aunt and uncle.

PRINCE: The prince thought it would be wrong to kill his own family, so they left the aunt and uncle in the dungeon that they had imprisoned him in.

KING: And the prince was made the rightful king.

PRINCE 2: And although Prince Tom had to return to his castle, they never forgot about each other.

PRINCE: The two princes fell in love, raised their kingdoms separately, but visited each other often

PRINCE 2: They eventually got married and raised the prince's cousin as their son.

NARRATOR: And they all lived happily ever after.

ALL: The end.

Chinese Food
by John Coons

CHARACTERS:
BEN   JOEY

SCENE: *Two guys on a bed, JOEY and BEN eating Chinese food. JOEY is in shorts and is shirtless, BEN is in pyjama pants and a t-shirt. JOEY begins, answering a question we don't hear.*

JOEY: Doubling my wardrobe.

BEN: Psh! You would say that. You're just lucky I'm about your height.

JOEY: Oh, it wasn't luck- it was a requirement. Blonde, brunet, bald, hairy, twink, black, white - whatever! Just give me someone with 30/32 jeans.

BEN: If I keep eating this General Tso's chicken, and I won't be able to fit into my 30/32 jeans...

JOEY: And you'll have to give them all to me- Muhahaha! It's all part of my evil plan.

BEN: World domination through Chinese food in bed in the afternoon.

JOEY: Mmm! Your turn.

BEN: (*Thinks it over, eats some more rice*) The massages.

JOEY: Because of what it leads to?

BEN: Hah! No! (*Smiles*) Not that I don't enjoy what they usually lead to... but, I mean, at the end of a long day, when I'm just dead, and I just fall down on the bed, face in the pillow... and then you come and sigh and shake your head, and then you give me a long, hard massage. Guys aren't afraid to really dig in, you know?

JOEY: (*With fake modesty*) Well, thank you very much, sir! I live to serve.

BEN: But... I mean, I love those, but...

JOEY: But....?

BEN: Clothes? You can buy more clothes. And a massage? You can buy one of those too.

JOEY: Hey, you asked what I liked the most about having a boyfriend.

BEN: Yeah, I should have remembered who I was asking... (*Grins*)

(*JOEY smacks him with a pillow*)
BEN (*Laughing*): Hey! Watch the rice! Collateral damage!

JOEY: Having someone to hit with a pillow. That's what I like!

BEN: I'm clearly in an abusive relationship.

JOEY: Took the words right from my mouth.

BEN (*Makes a face at JOEY*): Do you want me to go first?

(*JOEY gestures for him to continue*)

BEN: I think, for me. It's having someone who knows what you've gone through, because he's gone through it too- shitty high school years, coming out to friends and family. And it's more than just the shared traumatic experience of growing up gay... it's the highs of it too. Knowing that you understand what being with another guy means, how much I don't have to say out loud. And knowing that because you get me, you won't think any of my little fears or things I worry about are trivial. I don't feel judged for worrying about wearing the right clothes to work, or having lunch with my dad or... you know. That understanding, I guess.

(*JOEY thinks on this, eating some more.*)

JOEY: Finding someone you could spend all day waking up next to. I would be fine with just taking a bunch of short naps, so I could spend all day waking up, rolling over, and seeing you with bed head and a dopey grin.

BEN: Understanding and waking up all day.

JOEY: Good enough?

BEN: Good enough.

JOEY: Happy Thanksgiving, Ben.

BEN: Happy Thanksgiving, Joey.

(*They share a short kiss over the Chinese food, not even putting down their chopsticks. They smile and go back to eating. FADE TO BLACK.*)

Him, Her, & Me
By Madelyn James

Before… before I ever told her:
I didn't understand what I was supposed to do. Sure, she was pretty.
Sure, I remembered all of her likes and dislikes. But isn't that what
best friends are like? Our relationship seemed so much… so different.
Well, at least *my* relationship to her. She was so beautiful. So funny.
Every friendly handhold. I was happy just hugging her. Making all
of her worries go away. Wrapping my arms around her tiny frame.
Getting tinier, and I didn't know why. That worried me a little. I
listened to her breathe and saw her so at ease. Like when she rested
her head on my lap while we were watching movies. I'd gently brush
the stray hairs away from her face. Watch her—just breathing.

And there was him. They had been dating since I could remember.
Why was I so upset when she went to him? They were in a relationship, right? I liked him. He was nice. He made great desserts. Once he
made us brownies, ice cream, and fudge in a jar. It was so good! He
would invite the two of us out for a night on the town. He was good
for her. He could give her everything I couldn't. But at least she had
both a best friend and a boyfriend.

But wait. She left him? For me? No. For herself. But she wasn't alone.
Never alone. Because then there was another. Another him. But this
time something was different. I felt slowly exiled. I knew there would
never be an us. Why should there be? We're best friends or were best
friends. I shouldn't have felt this way. But she's so close. No! This
was wrong. She's…a she. This couldn't be real. Then why was I so…
jealous?

After… after I told her:

I felt like a bad person. I've never been convicted of a crime. I've never even been kicked out of school. But this made me feel like a bad person. Things fell apart. I made her uncomfortable. Was I a threat to him? I wasn't trying to steal her from him. I just wanted to keep a little piece of her—just her friendship. But with him there was no room for me.

I regretted telling her how I felt. I regretted every action, every word. Her. I got physically sick with fear. Fear of rejection, exile, hate. I wanted to crawl into a hole and disappear every time I got that look.

Now…
It's been months. And you know what? I take back nothing. If I could relive each day, good and bad, I wouldn't change a goddamn thing. I had my chance with her. At least I had my chance.

I don't love her but I do care. She can live her life. If she needs me, I'll be right here. Not waiting, but here. I miss the old friendship, but things are fitting into place for me. I'll find my way. My journey with her just made it a little easier. There will be another her and someday an us.

The Rules
by Alice Hofgren and Madelyn James

CHARACTERS:
CHARLOTTE   MAGGIE

CHARLOTTE: *(To audience)* Hi, I'm Charlotte, and there's this girl. Maggie. She's pretty awesome. I've known her for a few months and I'm thinking about going out on a limb here. I'm gonna ask her out. Seriously, I will this time. I've got this nice restaurant all picked out — here she comes!

(MAGGIE unfreezes.)

MAGGIE: Hey Charlotte!

CHARLOTTE: Hi!

(Pause.)

MAGGIE: …What's up?

CHARLOTTE: Oh! Um, I was wondering if maybe, if you aren't busy, we could probably, if you want, possibly, go see, like, a flick or something. Both of us. With me. Together.

MAGGIE: A flick?

CHARLOTTE: A movie. A film. A movie. Or something.

MAGGIE: Now?

CHARLOTTE: No, this Saturday. And we could also, maybe, get a bite to eat or something?

MAGGIE: Sure, sounds fun.

(MAGGIE freezes.)

CHARLOTTE: I'll text you the deets!

CHARLOTTE: *(To audience)* We went to see *Pirates of the Caribbean 13: Attack of the Whale Shark* followed by a lovely dinner at the Pasta Sub Sushi Hut. That is when I decided to pop the question.

(MAGGIE unfreeezes.)

MAGGIE: That was a strange movie, maybe next time I can choose.

CHARLOTTE: Next time?

MAGGIE: Yeah, this was fun, I'd love to do it again sometime.

CHARLOTTE: Do you want to… bemygirlfriend?

MAGGIE: What?

CHARLOTTE: Will you be my girlfriend?

(Pause.)

MAGGIE: I mean this nicely, but we have only been on one date. Maybe we should wait a few more dates—I'll call you tonight.

(MAGGIE freezes.)

CHARLOTTE: I didn't want to admit it, but she was right. I didn't really know her. We did go on a couple more dates—and every time I saw her, I liked her even more. And when we were out for a walk one night…

(MAGGIE unfreezes.)

MAGGIE: Yes.

CHARLOTTE: Yes what?

MAGGIE: I'll be your girlfriend.

CHARLOTTE: What if I changed my mind?

MAGGIE: Did you change your mind?

CHARLOTTE: No.

MAGGIE: Would you like to be my girlfriend?

CHARLOTTE: Yes!

MAGGIE: Okay, Miss Hard-to-Get. But there have to be some ground rules. Rule number one: We need to tell each other if something is wrong between us. None of this "Oh it's nothing" crap.

CHARLOTTE: Okay that's easy enough.

MAGGIE: Whoa! Slow your roll there, bub. I'm not finished. Rule number two: I want to make this work but we should not sacrifice our own happiness for the sake of the other person. No martyr-y B.S. We each need to be happy to be happy together. Yes?

CHARLOTTE: I agree. I might not have said it out loud at this moment—but I like this all your cards on the table approach. Carry on.

MAGGIE: Rule number three: No movies with Sarah Jessica Parker in them.

CHARLOTTE: What?! She's awesome!

MAGGIE: Or Kristin Stewart.

CHARLOTTE: Really?!

MAGGIE. Don't make me regret this.

CHARLOTTE. I want to add one.

MAGGIE: To the ACTOR list or the rule list?

CHARLOTTE: Rule list.

MAGGIE: Absolutely.

CHARLOTTE: Rule number four: Monogamy. I have nothing against open relationships, but they're not for me.

MAGGIE. Thought that one was a given. Yes, good rule. Anything else?

CHARLOTTE. Nope.

MAGGIE. Commence social media relationship status updates.

(Both laugh. MAGGIE freezes.)

CHARLOTTE: *(To the audience)* Things started to get more intimate. Every time I was around Maggie I had these big metal butterflies fluttering around in my stomach. Then we went to the drive-in.

MAGGIE: *(Unfreezes)* I've never been to a drive-in before. I didn't even know there was one around here.

CHARLOTTE: Neither did I, my friend told me about it and I thought it would be fun. Plus, I heard they have great corn dogs.

(Pause.)

MAGGIE: I bet you ten bucks Ryan Gosling kisses at least two women in this movie.

CHARLOTTE: You're on. *(Pause)* I really like your hair like that.

MAGGIE: Thanks, I really like your… necklace.

(Over the next few lines they bring their faces closer to each other.)

CHARLOTTE: You have pretty eyes.

MAGGIE: Thanks. I like your freckles.

CHARLOTTE: Thanks. You're really close to my face.

MAGGIE: You're really close to *my* face.

(Pause.)

CHARLOTTE & MAGGIE: *(Together)* Can I kiss you?

(MAGGIE freezes.)

CHARLOTTE: *(To audience)* Okay, you don't need to see this...She said yes. I said yes. We kissed! It was great! I felt electrified, Maggie said she saw fireworks. Things progressed and we just kept checking in with each other to make sure that in the heat of the moment we were on the same page. You know, it is sort of sexy to ask someone what she wants or come up with creative suggestions. Anyway, we are still dating today and it is because of this communication and our ground rules that we were able to keep a healthy relationship for two and a half years. Especially Rule three. Rule three is very important. Sometimes we disagree about things, but by being honest and aware of the other person's feelings we are able to make our relationship stronger. I'm planning on taking her to the new *Pirates of the Caribbean* movie.

(MAGGIE Unfreezes)

MAGGIE: No!

CHARLOTTE: You're frozen; you're not supposed to be able to hear these parts.

MAGGIE: Well I can.

CHARLOTTE: It's supposed to be the best one yet.

MAGGIE: Can we please pick one together?

CHARLOTTE: Okay. What about the new *Twilight* movie? I think Kristin Stewart gets staked by a new species of werewolf zombies who glow in the dark within the first few minutes so it might be an exception to the rule...

MAGGIE: Maybe...maybe. *(They exit together.)*

Once
by Emma Blackman-Mathis for Dreams of Hope

Once, on a white piece of paper with blue lines
I wrote a poem about a dog
Because that was my favorite animal
And my teacher gave me an A
And I told her I loved her
And I went home to my mom and dad
Because they both lived here then
And they were both so proud of me
And that night, my daddy tucked me in
And cuddled me
And I asked him why he tucks me in after my brothers
And he said so he could be with me the longest
And I felt so loved

Once, on the pages of a book
I read a story about a little girl and her family
And it made me sad, because her family was broken and little
And I wanted to share my family with her
But I knew I couldn't
So all I could do was feel bad
And I told my mom and she told me it was ok
And I felt a million times better
That was the year they started fighting
And I would just sit up in my room
And cry
Because I didn't want my daddy to leave
He was my hero

Once, on a little scrap of paper I drew a picture of a happy family
And I started to cry
Because it made me remember how we used to be
Before my dad moved down the street

And I wanted so badly to run to him
I wanted him to walk in and we could all be happy again
But I knew that he didn't abandon me
And when I saw him that night, I told him I loved him
One million times and more
And just hugging him made me feel better
I knew he would always be there

Once, when I was marking times as the runners came in during
     practice
I thought about love
And how I knew I wasn't like all of the other little girls
Because every time I saw her
I got that little bit of excitement
And I wanted to sigh about her like they did about boys
But I didn't know what to do about it
So that day I made a decision
And I told her about me being gay
And she said she had figured it out
And then I told everyone how I was
But not specifically who I loved at that point
And I felt so
Freed
And I told my parents
And my mom was so happy for me
And my dad and his girlfriend were proud
And everything fit for once

Once, on two sheets of paper that were scribbled on and smudged
I wrote my first love letter
To the first person I ever came out to
I wrote it to her
Because it was about her
And I wanted her
Even though I knew I couldn't have her
I wanted her to know how I felt about her
And on a sheet of paper quite like those
She told me she hated me
And that she had used me
And that she never even cared
She left me broken
She left me whimpering and huddled in a corner
But I stayed true to myself

And once, when my first real girlfriend and I were face to face
I told her that I loved her so deeply
And that love would never go away
But we couldn't work
We both cried about this
And it still hurts
But I have to start drawing my lines
And it starts with those thin little blue ones on that white piece of
    paper

And between these new lines
I realize that my dad is still there
And that he will always be my hero
And my mom still loves me
And I will still be able to talk to her
Because I know I still get sad about the fact that my dad doesn't live
    with me anymore
And I know that I still feel bad about the little girl with her broken
    family
But I also know that the family of the people I love
Love me back
And this is what I have
And that is what I want
The love
Between the lines
And the love on the lines
Because love makes a family

"Vision without action is daydream.
Action without vision is nightmare."
- Japanese Proverb

Action

An Out & Allied DIY
by Meghan Brodie, Ph.D.

Perhaps you are planning an Out & Allied performance and want to include your own pieces and/or those written by your community members. This is a great idea. The following is a mini DIY module outlining how you might create a performance piece by adapting your own story for the stage.

1. Write down the story you want to tell. Or, better yet, get a group of people together and host a writing session. Snacks help.
2. Consider how you want to tell the story. Does it lend itself to a monologue format? A multiple-person scene? A poem? A song? From whose perspective will the story be told? Would the content be best expressed as a comedy? A drama? Because we frequently write from our own experiences, our first instincts might be to craft our experiences in the form of monologues. Monologues, however, are not always the most appropriate dramatic form for every story. While individual storytelling is valuable, if you are planning on presenting multiple pieces, it helps to include different types of material: monologues, scenes, songs, poems, etc.
3. Think about what you want an audience to take away from the piece. What do you hope audience members will learn or feel or even <u>do</u> after seeing your performance?
4. Give your performance piece a title so it can be included in a program and on your resume.

Here's an example of how to transform a story into a performance piece. First, let's look at the story I want to tell. I thought about my own experience coming out to my grandmother and recorded my thoughts:

I'm not a religious person, but my grandmother was. She was a second generation Catholic Italian-American. I remember her going to mass every Sunday and supporting her church in any way she could. She gathered food for food drives, bought gifts for children who might not otherwise find anything under their Christmas trees, and baked for the priests and nuns around holidays. If she and my grandfather had anything in their house that they didn't need, she donated it to the church — including the suit in which my grandfather married her. My grandmother prayed every night and had a rich religious life. So when I fell in love with a woman, I didn't really know how my grandmother would respond.

The idea of my grandmother praying for me because I was gay pained me — I didn't want to change but I also didn't want my grandmother to worry about me or my soul. I don't tend to think of Catholics as particularly gay-friendly. I take issue with the Church's position on contraception, sexuality, women's place in the church…let's just say it's an extensive list. My views were not a surprise to my grandmother. We never argued. But I was uneasy about telling my grandmother I was gay. I didn't want her to have to choose between me and the church that was a part of her daily life.

Despite all of my reservations, not telling my grandmother was not an option. We were a closely-knit family and bringing my lesbian girlfriend to the next family get together or holiday gathering would not go unnoticed. So I told my grandmother. She wasn't angry. She wasn't upset. She was happy I was happy. And when my girlfriend was with my family for Christmas, I was surprised that my grandmother distributed gifts to each of her grandchildren and my girlfriend. My grandmother loved me and extended her love to the woman who eventually became my life partner.

It never occurred to my grandmother that she needed to choose between her Catholic faith and me. Despite Church teachings, my grandmother accepted me for who I was and I don't believe she ever prayed for me to be anyone other than the lesbian granddaughter I was. I realize that my grandmother's response to my sexuality might not be common among Catholics, but it gave me hope that faith communities might follow my grandmother's lead and privilege love above all else.

So I have my general story. The easiest approach to adapting this story for the stage would be to identify it as a monologue and have an actor share the story with an audience. While more of a challenge, converting this story into a multiple-person scene might give it more life, better engage an audience, and help audience members to identify with both my story as well as my grandmother's story. Although the subject matter is certainly serious—coming out can be a defining moment in one's life as well as the lives of those to whom one comes out—my coming out experience was not exceptionally frightening or sad. Given that the story has a positive conclusion and there are a few elements that could be portrayed with humor (like my grandmother's inclination to give everything, including my grandfather's wedding suit, to the church), it might be worthwhile to try to turn this story into a comic scene without undermining the message I want to convey.

And what message do I want to convey to an audience? I need to have a sense of this before writing my comic scene. If possible, I would like my scene to communicate that despite stereotypes, those who are religious (in this case, Catholic) are not all homophobic and don't all believe that those who are queer (in terms of their sexuality, gender expression, etc.) are wrong or sick or sinful. On the contrary, many people of faith and entire faith communities support their queer friends and family members. I also want to point out that loving me didn't make my grandmother any less of a Catholic. Her faith was rooted in love and despite certain church teachings, my sexuality didn't present a problem for her. I guess she interpreted her faith a bit differently than the Catholic Church outlined it for her. My goal would be for a performance piece to communicate the possibility of embracing those who are different. I would like audience members to leave and think twice before assuming that members of faith communities might be predisposed to reject those leading queer lives. And, of course, I want to encourage members of faith communities to welcome and respect everyone regardless of their sex, gender expression, or sexuality.

And a title? I don't have one yet. I am hoping the scene, when it is complete, will yield a catchy title.

Here's the scene I wrote based on the story shared above:

CHARACTERS
ELLA
GRANDMA

SETTING: GRANDMA'S kitchen.

ELLA: *(Sitting at the kitchen table, talking to the audience)* This is my grandmother's kitchen. My grandmother is currently upstairs putting laundry in the dryer. She is going to come downstairs, probably offer me pretzels, and ask me about school.

(GRANDMA enters.)

GRANDMA: Hon, do you want some more pretzels? Cheese?

(GRANDMA freezes.)

ELLA: *(To the audience)* And cheese. I forgot about the cheese. Cheddar or havarti. She's Italian—she likes to feed people.

(GRANDMA unfreezes.)

GRANDMA: I have cheddar and havarti. And crackers.

ELLA: No thanks, I'm good right now.

(GRANDMA sits at the table.)

GRANDMA: How's school? When do you have to go back?

ELLA: It's good. I head back on Sunday.

GRANDMA: I made an extra batch of biscotti so you can take a tin back with you.

ELLA: Thanks. But you didn't have to do that. Thank you—I will ration them to last until Christmas.

(GRANDMA freezes.)

ELLA: *(To the audience)* Now I am thinking how on earth am I going to get from pretzels, havarti, and biscotti to the main event here? And she says:

(GRANDMA unfreezes.)

GRANDMA: It's okay I doubled the recipe—
(GRANDMA freezes.)

ELLA: *(To the audience)* A doubled recipe means she baked for her priest and/or the nuns.

(GRANDMA unfreezes.)

GRANDMA: —so I could take some to the nuns this Sunday.

ELLA: That's nice. I am sure they will love them as much as I do.

GRANDMA: They are doing a clothing drive for the next two Sundays so I thought I would bring some biscotti when I drop off a few bags of clothes.

ELLA: Is it true you donated Grandpa's suit from your wedding?

GRANDMA: Oh yes, I donated that years ago. I couldn't imagine he would be wearing it again. It was a really nice suit and I'm sure it went to a good home.

(GRANDMA freezes.)

ELLA: *(To the audience)* Okay, attempting a transition from pretzels and biscotti would have been easier than segueing from nuns and religious ceremonies, but it's now or never.

(GRANDMA unfreezes.)

ELLA: Hey Grandma, there was something I wanted to tell you.
GRANDMA: What is it, hon?

ELLA: Welllllll, I am pretty sure I'm gay.

(Beat.)

GRANDMA: Oh. Okay.

(GRANDMA freezes.)

ELLA: *(To the audience)* That's a bit tricky to read. "Oh. Okay."
"Oh okay I'm down with the gays?" or "oh okay I'll just start
praying the gay away right now?" Forging ahead...

(GRANDMA unfreezes.)

ELLA: I am sort of seeing this girl, Kate. She's really nice. She
lives in the city. I met her last year and we started emailing...
Anyway, I really like her. A lot. There is so much liking involved
that I love her.

GRANDMA: You know as long as you're happy that's all that
matters to me.

ELLA: But I don't want you thinking I am going to hell or worrying about me or praying for me anything.

GRANDMA: I pray for all of you, all of my children and grandchildren, every night.

ELLA: I meant I don't want you to pray for me because I'm gay.

GRANDMA: Why would I pray for you because you're gay?

ELLA: The last time I checked Catholics were not too keen on
the gays, Grandma.

GRANDMA: Well I don't think it matters. Who you love is no-body else's business. I don't see what the fuss is about. What's her name again?

ELLA: Kate.

GRANDMA: Is Kate coming to Christmas Eve? Does she like biscotti? I could send her a few of the biscotti I made for the nuns if you're going to see her before you go back to school. Do you think she'd like ricotta cheesecake? I'm thinking I might need to make three for Christmas this year.

ELLA: Grandma, you're pretty amazing. Do you think Grandpa will be okay with it?

GRANDMA: Oh yes, hon, don't worry. I'll tell him. Are you sure you don't want some cheese and crackers? Or maybe some pistachios?

ELLA: Pistachios sound good.

GRANDMA: I'll get them. I just put a new bag in the pantry this morning.

(GRANDMA exits.)

ELLA: *(To the audience)* You know I don't think most people's coming out experiences are quite this easy. "Grandma, I'm gay." "That's nice, hon. Do you want some pistachios?" I underes-timated her. And while I personally may not be fond of the Catholic Church and its position on contraception, sexuality, women — it's a long list — I have to admit that I was wrong to presuppose that my grandmother's reaction to my sexuality would be any different just because she is Catholic. Who's to say that one day the Catholic Church won't be a community of people just like my grandmother? One can hope.

END

That's the scene. It requires only a table and two chairs so it can be performed almost anywhere and with few resources. I changed my own name to create a little bit of distance between me and the character I created (who just so happens to be quite a bit like me). I changed my girlfriend's name because anytime I write about people I know, I try to protect their privacy by changing their names in my work. And while I don't remember every detail of the conversation I had with my grandmother and I ended up drawing upon a couple of conversations I had with her, the scene is an honest depiction of my grandmother's response to my coming out.

And a title? I decided on *Havarti & Pistachios*, a variation on a "before" (havarti) I told her and "after" (pistachios) I told her theme and a tribute to my grandmother's generosity and love.

Only an audience can decide if I achieved my goals and if this piece resonates with them. But I hope this mini module on adapting an Out & Allied story for the stage has inspired you to share your experiences. You are welcome to use the story or its scene adaptation in your own production of pieces from this collection.

Introduction and Storytelling
Gayrilla Theatre Troupe

CHARACTERS:

ORANGE	BLUE	PURPLE
RED	YELLOW	GREEN

Editors Note: *Here's an example of a group introducing themselves and their development process. You can use this as a template for how you introduce your own program.*

Introduction:

ORANGE: Hello and thank you. It is my pleasure to introduce you to the Gayrilla Theatre Project.

PURPLE: *(Thinking)* It's like Gorilla Theatre

BLUE: *(Thinking)* But with gays…

PURPLE and BLUE: Gayrilla!

ORANGE: Right, so the idea for using theatre with Riot Youth came about a number of years ago.

PURPLE: Hey, hanging out and eating pizza is cool and all, but I wanted to MOVE! *(They do a little dance)*

BLUE: Yeah, plus I needed to get stuff off my chest.

PURPLE: Yeah, but in a really creative way.

BLUE and PURPLE: Hmmm *(Thinking)*…

ORANGE: So Riot Youth decided…

BLUE: We want to do theatre!

PURPLE: And we want it to be socially relevant!

BLUE: And we want it to be about our lives!

PURPLE: And we want to change the world!

ORANGE: So Riot Youth started doing some theatre! Then one day, a teen came to Riot Youth and told them about an idea he had for a survey project.

PURPLE: Riot Youth should do a survey.

EVERYONE: A survey! (Jump)

BLUE: We could use the survey to find out about other queer youth.

PURPLE: And then use theatre to help tell people about the results of the survey.

ORANGE: Hey, but I bet you'll need some funding.

PURPLE: Hi! I'm Liberty Hill and the Arcus Foundation, and U of M's Arts of Citizenship Program, how about a little cash?

ORANGE and BLUE: Cha-ching!

ORANGE: And then maybe you could perform for members of the community, your peers and people in the Ann Arbor School System.

ORANGE: So that brings us to today. Gayrilla Theatre is not about producing big Broadway quality shows. It is about Storytelling plain and simple. The youth you see here represent their own stories…

BLUE: That did not happen to you!

PURPLE: It totally did!

ORANGE: And they represent the voices of other queer youth from Riot Youth, from Ann Arbor, from all around Washtenaw County.

PURPLE: That did not happen to you!

BLUE: No but it happened to someone at my school.

PURPLE: Wow…

ORANGE: So now we give you Gayrilla Theatre…

BLUE: "LGBTQ Youth and Visibility…"

PURPLE: Good title.

BLUE: I know right?

Storytelling:

GREEN: Part 1: Storytelling

SETTING: *Members of RY are spaced on the stage with backs turned. One by one they turn around to face the audience as they speak. Each person has a "sound bite"; one phrase that gives an example of a time they have felt, invisible or unsafe.*

RED: LGBTQ Youth have stories to tell.

PURPLE: Um…mom, dad we need to talk.

GREEN: So yeah, so sleepovers have become really awkward…

YELLOW: When my parents reference my future relationships, they always say '(boyfriend/girlfriend)' by accident.

BLUE: Then his dad said: The only thing worse than my son joining the army would be my son being a fag.

RED: They have stories to tell about feeling invisible.

PURPLE: I think if we have to hear about straight sex in health class, they should have to hear about gay sex… Do they think we don't need that information too? How am I supposed to learn about being healthy and safe in my relationship? Do they even realize I am in the room?

ORANGE: Only 3.31% of the entire sample says that queer health issues are given a thorough overview. Inadequate coverage of queer health related issues marginalizes 10.5% of the students surveyed and leaves them insufficiently informed about their own health.

GREEN: At school they don't see *me*. They don't understand how my days are, how I view the world. They just don't get it.

ORANGE: Over 1,000 students took the Riot Youth Climate Survey in high schools across Ann Arbor. Of these, 17 identified outside the traditional male/female binary.

YELLOW: I was tired of feeling like the only gay person, tired of being verbally abused, but I didn't know where to go. So I hid. I felt like I basically didn't exist ... I was hiding from the world.

BLUE: Where is my community? I don't see myself on TV, in my books, in examples in class. There is a movement and my community has a history. Where is it?

ORANGE: Queer students (grouping together lesbian, bisexual, gay, transgender, queer and questioning students) represented 10.5% of the students surveyed.

YELLOW: I become invisible to protect myself. The last thing I want to do is draw more attention to myself. So no, I won't be attending the pep rally, I'd like to have a harassment free afternoon, thank you.
RED: Stories about feeling and being unsafe.

GREEN: I don't feel safe walking to school every day.

BLUE: They pelted me with fruit in the cafeteria.

PURPLE: I had a bible thrown at me on my school bus.

YELLOW: They called me a (fag/dyke) in the middle of class.

PURPLE: They called me a (fag/dyke) in the middle of class.

GREEN: They called me an "it" in the middle of class.

PURPLE, GREEN, and YELLOW: The teacher didn't do anything.

GREEN: When I told administrators that the bathrooms were an unsafe place for me, they told me to use the nurse's bathroom on the other end of the school. Like I was the problem.

BLUE: A bunch of hockey players followed me out of school and ran me off the road. I skipped school for a week after that.

ORANGE: Queer students feel significantly less safe in school, and in public restrooms than their non-queer counterparts, based on their sexual orientation, gender identification and gender expression. They were also physically and verbally harassed significantly more than non-queer students. On average 94% of non-queer students felt safe, but only 62% of queer students felt safe.

RED: LGBTQ youth have stories about not being able to move.

PURPLE: I can't hug another girl without people staring or whispering.

BLUE: I told her that it was a phase so that it wouldn't be awkward between us. Like I un-came out. I came out. Then went back in.

GREEN: I'm scared to walk to my classes. I take the long route and risk being late…or I don't go at all.

PURPLE: I don't even know if he was gay. They tormented him just because they thought he walked kind of feminine.

GREEN: I was just walking to class and this (guy/girl) comes out of nowhere, getting in my face, like "Hey did you just check out my (girlfriend/boyfriend)"?

RED: They have stories about not being able to speak.

PURPLE: I was afraid it was just going to slip out, like when I was giving announcements in the morning: So, there's a cross country meeting in the lecture court and I'm gay.

RED: So I did tell my counselor about all the harassment. How I can't concentrate in class because of it, and she said, maybe you should just transfer to (Community/the alternative school). I don't bring it up anymore.

YELLOW: My friends always talk about (boys/girls) but get all quiet when I talk about another girl in the same way.

PURPLE: You feel like you can't talk to anyone because you are afraid of what they might say, who they might tell... and what their reaction might be. Do you know what it feels like to carry that around with you?

BLUE: I couldn't compliment my friends. Every word for pretty sounded gay.

RED: Stories about hearing their identity used as an insult...as the worst thing to be.

YELLOW: And then she said: "That's so gay."

BLUE: And he was like: "Hey! No homo!"

PURPLE: Like being gay is funny...a joke.

RED: She told me to chill out.

GREEN: To quit being so damn P.C.

BLUE: After all, it's not an insult to gay people.

EVERYONE: They are just words.

ORANGE: Students responded that they often hear homophobic and biphobic language. Many other non-queer students don't understand why this language is harmful.

YELLOW: Why do I always have to be the one to explain that those kinds of words are damaging to me? Why do I always have to be the one when...

GREEN: My friends.

PURPLE: My teachers.

RED: My principals.

BLUE: My parents.

YELLOW: When they hear it too…and don't speak up?

ORANGE: According to the survey, teachers and staff intervene rarely in instances of harassment based on sexual orientation or transgender identities. Students are even less likely to intervene. Some students explained why: "If I defend gays, people might see me as gay."

RED: LBGTQ youth have stories and with those stories they have questions. Questions for their teachers;
PURPLE: Why can't you hear them making fun of me?

GREEN: Why don't you do something?

BLUE: How am I supposed to concentrate when they won't leave me alone?

YELLOW: Are you seriously giving me a hard time about being late? Do you have any idea of what it's like for me to walk down the halls?

BLUE: Why are there only 4 sentences about gay history in my 800 page text book?!

YELLOW: How do I know if it's safe to talk to you? How do I know you won't hate me?

RED: How come I got a perfect score on my A.C.T, but you don't tell me about our GSA because you're afraid they might brainwash me gay. Do you think I can't think for myself?

ORANGE: Teachers "rarely" discuss LGBTQ history and cultural significance and rarely use inclusive examples in class. Lack of examples increases feelings of isolation, lack of representation leads to more ignorance which leads to mistreatment of queer people.

GREEN: When you talk about the value of diversity, does that include me?

RED: Questions for their counselors and administrators.

YELLOW: How can you help me.

PURPLE: And protect me.

YELLOW and PURPLE: If you can't accept me?

BLUE: Why do I feel like I am the problem? Like I'm "asking for it" by being myself?

YELLOW: How come when I tell you I don't feel comfortable here, you tell me to try and graduate early?

ORANGE: Queer students on average felt only somewhat comfortable talking to school
administrators, counselors, and teachers on issues of sexual orientation, gender identity and gender expression.

RED: Can you help me create a safer community?

BLUE: Do I deserve less of an education because of my sexual orientation?

GREEN: Because of my gender identity?

PURPLE: Don't I have a right to feel safe?

YELLOW: No matter what your personal beliefs?

EVERYONE: Don't I???

RED: Questions for their peers;

PURPLE: Why do you get to have a safe space, but I don't?

GREEN: Everyone is different. Why can't you just accept me?

YELLOW: I am not hurting you. Why can't you just leave me alone?

RED: And for you...

(At this point all of RY turn downstage and begin walking toward the audience. They all speak over the top of each other throwing questions at the audience.)

RED: Can we work together to find solutions to keep me safe? Are you going to tell my parents?

BLUE: I want to go to a college that has good support for LGBT students, can you help me research? How do I know that I can trust you?

YELLOW: Can you talk to my teacher with me? Are you going to listen to me?

ORANGE: My parents kicked me out of the house when I told them I was gay, can you help me? Are you going to listen without judging me?

PURPLE: I need to tell you about an issue I am having with my girlfriend, will you listen? Where can I find allies in the school system?

GREEN: And most importantly...

EVERYONE: How will you support us?

GREEN: We tell our stories because we want you to know how it feels to be us. We tell our stories because if people know who we are, it might help keep others safe.

YELLOW: We tell our stories because as LGBTQ youth we are 3 times more likely to commit suicide, feel significantly less safe using school bathrooms, less safe talking to our teachers, counselors and administrators, and are more likely to be physically and verbally harassed on our way to school, to class, to our homes

EVERYONE: Even in Ann Arbor.

ORANGE: We tell our stories because we feel isolated, scared and disenfranchised. Because we are GOOD STUDENTS who are skipping classes, arriving late, failing to concentrate, not joining after school activities, trying to graduate early, dropping out, not "realizing our aspirations," our potential....

EVERYONE: Because WE are an at risk population!

GREEN: We tell our stories because we have to... We tell our stories to keep from being invisible...

RED: I'm Red.

ORANGE: I'm Orange.

YELLOW: I'm Yellow.

GREEN: I'm Green.

BLUE: I'm Blue.

PURPLE: I'm Purple.

PURPLE: We tell our stories because we want to change the world. Because...

ORANGE: We.

PURPLE: Are.

YELLOW: Riot.

BLUE: Youth.

EVERYONE: And we are here to recruit you!

Into Action
by Anonymous Teachers

CHARACTERS:

BYSTANDER 1   BYSTANDER 2
BYSTANDER 3   BYSTANDER 4
VICTIM   BULLY

STAGING DIRECTIONS: Adapt the performance for the number of actors, and change to any bystander scenario. Begin together in one frozen image, representing a situation in which each has the opportunity to choose to be an ally. Each is frozen in a physical position representing how they feel at that moment in time. Image in each scene established, every individual says a word in character that further represents how they are feeling. The three central players then break their frozen position to deliver a monologue that answers the questions: "What's at stake?", "What's important to you right now?", and "What's in your way/what do you want?"

After each short monologue, they then resume their former frozen state. When all have completed these, the characters as one make a physical shift to represent a change in their actions and thoughts. The movement reflects the process each character goes through as they decide what or what not to do in the situation. The characters then say a new word, *in character*, representing their new state of mind.

Below are sample monologues, and descriptions of characters positions within the image.

BYSTANDER 1 moves from "Fear" → "Helping." This bystander is standing the furthest from the victim and represents an uncertain ally. Her first pose is cowering, unsure as to whether she should step in and help the victim. Her second pose is more certain, and she is moving decidedly towards the bully, ready to intervene.

BYSTANDER 2 moves from "Not Accepting" → "Ignorance." This bystander is watching the bullying and approves of what is happening. She appears ready to join in the bullying. This is explained by her second word, "ignorance." She does not know anything about homosexuality and her ignorance translates to cruelty.

BYSTANDER 3 (friend of BYSTANDER 2) moves from "Disrupting" → "Redirecting." This bystander does not agree with the bullying, but neither is she ready to intercede. She is merely trying to prevent her friend (BYSTANDER 2) from joining in. By her second action, she has grown more proactive, and is trying to physically move her friend away from the situation.

BYSTANDER 4 moves from "Get over it" → "Supporting." This bystander happens to be a friend of the victim, but her first pose is very unsympathetic. Her second pose, however, represents a willing-ness to intercede on her friend's behalf.

VICTIM moves from "Powerless" → "Acceptance." The victim is sitting, therefore physically lower down than the bully, and is covering her face and trying to appear as small as possible in the first pose. By the second pose, the action on the part of some of the bystanders has empowered her, and she feels accepted rather than rejected. This new self-confidence is reflected in her more upright stance.

BULLY moves from "Popular" → "Ignore." The bully originally has a position of power over the victim, as she is confronting the victim head on and is standing over the seated victim. However, due to the actions of the bystanders, the bully loses power in her second pose, and decides to turn away from the victim, representing that she has now decided to ignore the victim.

MONOLOGUES:

BYSTANDER 4: Why can't she just get over it? There's no need to take this so hard! You can't let them see that it matters to you — it just shows your vulnerability!"

VICTIM: I feel alone, powerless. No one cares about me. My friends are gone. I can only see myself the way they see me: ugly, weird, unlovable. I want to be myself *and* be accepted. I want others to see the value in me."

BULLY: I want an audience, some power. I lack self-confidence, so the more pain I can inflict...well, the better for me. By doing this, I can gain popularity, and assuage my fears of appearing weak, or unmasculine. Only bystanders can stand in my way, and they don't appear to be doing anything."

Authors Note: *Understanding a situation and the personal motivations of the people involved is essential to interfering successfully and stopping bullying and harassment. This type of scene helps actors and audience members to break a scene down and examine the different possible outcomes given each character's wants and needs.*

For more information on how to do Image Theatre, we recommend:
- Theatre for Community, Conflict and Dialogue by Michael Rohd (1998)
- Games for Actors and Non Actors by Augusto Boal (1992)

Coming Out: An Orientation Skit

Collaboratively created by Sharon Green, Allen Rigby, Dylan Goodman, and the Davidson College Health Advisors from 2011-2013

CHARACTERS:

ALLEN, our protagonist	LIZ, a high school student
PETER, his roommate	DYLAN, a high school student
JANE, Peter's best high school friend	STUDENT 1, a male high school student
HALL COUNSELOR, at the college	STUDENT 2, a female high school student.
HALLMATE #1	HALLMATE #2, a homophobic tool

STAGING NOTE: The names for the high school students can be changed. It is recommended that a woman play HALLMATE #2. 6 Chairs were the only props used for this scene.

SETTING: *At open, a high school scene, before class. Two rows of seats, students in chairs. STUDENTS 1 & 2 cozy in the back row, possibly boyfriend/girlfriend, possibly making out. DYLAN and LIZ in front row. Other students possible.*

DYLAN: Yo, Liz.

LIZ: Dylan, I'm not going to prom with you.

DYLAN: Oh, God! That was like a week ago!

LIZ: Dylan, you ask me that like every day.

DYLAN: Liz, there's something on my - Oh! It's my senioritis! You're getting it! Oh, my God! It's contagious!

LIZ: *(Addressing the entire classroom)* Guys, I forgot to tell you. Yesterday, I was walking to my car, and guess who I saw in the parking lot.

DYLAN: That skank Britney?

LIZ: No, it was Allen... our favorite. (*Grumbles from all students*). Oh, but it's fine. He was just making out... with a boy.

('Eews' from all students)

(ALLEN enters and tries to sit next to LIZ. She blocks the seat.)

LIZ: Not today... sorry.

(ALLEN tries another seat.)

STUDENT 1: I don't think so, faggot.

STUDENT 2: Nice shirt, Allen. You're looking especially fag-tastic today.

(High school action freezes. ALLEN walks downstage and addresses the audience.)

ALLEN: Because of experiences like that, I didn't know what I wanted to do at Davidson. I really wanted to be comfortable and be able to be out to my friends and the rest of campus, so that I could have "the best four years of my life." But, I didn't want to deal with stuff like that (*gestures upstage*) for four years. Little did I know, my roommate also had some apprehensions.

(ALLEN and students leave the stage. 2 new characters, JANE and PETER, ALLEN's roommate, enter.)

JANE: So, I bought about three hundred clothes hangers; I'm hoping that's going to be enough.

PETER: Three hundred clothes hangers!?

JANE: I think I'm going to color coordinate by season.

PETER: You don't even have that many clothes.

JANE: I definitely do have that many. Oh, I got my roommate!

PETER: Yeah, me too.

JANE: So, I looked at her pictures on Facebook, I've checked her Tumblr, she tweets like a boss, and her Pinterest... all I can say is that we are definitely "pintred" spirits.

PETER: So you're like...stalking her!?

JANE: Her Vines are HILARIOUS.

PETER: You're such a creep.

JANE: Didn't you stalk yours?

PETER: No! I'm not a creep like you.

JANE: No, it's totally socially acceptable. You stalk them before you meet them.

PETER: Uh... I don't know.

JANE: Just pull up his Facebook. Right here. Right now. Here we go.

PETER: Alright.

JANE: You just need to know a little about him, that's all.

PETER: Well, his name is Allen.

JANE: Allen from where?

PETER: Alabama. Allen from Alabama.

JANE: What's his profile picture?

PETER: I mean, he's just chillin'.

JANE: Is he in a sunflower field? Oh my God. Oh my God!

PETER: What!?

JANE: Your roommate's totally gay.

PETER: Whoa, whoa. What!?

JANE: You're roommate is GAY.

PETER: Because he's in a sunflower field?

JANE: Precisely.

PETER: Maybe he's just artsy?

JANE: Maybe he's just gay. Just...look at his favorite TV shows. Read them out to me.

PETER: Let's see... Glee

JANE: Hmmph.

PETER: Grey's Anatomy...

JANE: Mmm..

PETER: Sex and the City...

JANE: Wait for it...

PETER: Will & Grace?

JANE: I told you. My gaydar is impeccable.

PETER: No. Listen. This is why you don't stalk people on the Internet. Just because you see a picture of flowers...

JANE: No, no, no. He's gay. I'm gonna need you to accept it and move forward so we can make a plan.

PETER: A plan? What do you mean?

JANE: Well, you can't just walk into your room like, "Hey, gay roommate!" You've got to formulate a plan of action.

PETER: You mean, like to see if he's gay or not?

JANE: Yes, exactly.

PETER: Um, okay. Well, you're a girl, right?

JANE: Uh, yeah...

PETER: Well, why don't you get on your Facebook and hit him up, and be like, "Oh my God, you're so cute!" or whatever.

JANE: Like, flirt with him?

PETER: Yeah!

JANE: Ok... so I'm going to do this for you, because we've been through a lot together. You're my bro. But this is creepy... even for my standards.

(JANE exits. PETER walks downstage to address the audience.)

PETER: I would be lying if I said I wasn't nervous about having a gay roommate. I'm from a small town in the northeast and all the guys I hung out with were always into girls. I'd never really even met a gay person before. I didn't know how I would react if Allen were to come out to me once we got to campus. I was worried that, even if I became friends with Allen and really liked him, people would think that I was gay, because I was associated with him. When we actually met a few weeks later, I didn't want to jump to conclusions, but I was kinda nervous that there was something he wasn't telling me.

(PETER exits. Scene Change: A hall meeting in a male freshman dorm.)

HALL COUNSELOR: *(with extreme enthusiasm)* Ok, ok everybody. Alrighty. That was a riveting discussion of the Code of Responsibility. Now, we're gonna finish off with some icebreakers. Alright, so the way this is gonna work is we're gonna go around the room, and we're gonna say our name, our home state, and our favorite brand of toothpaste. Ok, who wants to go first? *(Pause)* Ok, I'll go! My name is Bradley, I'm from Michigan, and my favorite brand of toothpaste is... Colgate. Anyone else? *(HALLMATE 1 raises hand, is ignored by HALL COUNSELOR)* Anyone? *(HALLMATE 1 persists)* Ok, go!

HALLMATE 1: Hi, I'm Jack, I'm from South Carolina, and my favorite brand of toothpaste is...Sensodyne!

HALLMATE 2: Okay, I think I speak for everyone when I say this hall meeting has gone on for entirely too long. It's unnecessary, and I think we all have a lot of stuff to do.

HALL COUNSELOR: That's a great suggestion and (*looks around the room*) consensus! I'm glad we're working together on this! Thanks, guys. Great first hall meeting. One more thing: no alcohol on the hall. All love, no hate. Peace, guys, peace! Gonna be a great year!

HALLMATE 1: Hey, Bradley, how do I get a 4.0?

HALL COUNSELOR: Sorry, it's quiet hours. And that's impossible.

(*Both exit.*)

PETER: Dude, if I have to sit through another one of those meetings...

ALLEN: I know, seriously.

PETER: ...my head's going to explode. I mean, toothpaste!? Seriously?

ALLEN: I know. I'm never buying Colgate again. Ever.

PETER: Me neither. Jeez. Anyways, have you seen the girls on 2nd Schmelk?

ALLEN: Um, yeah. I've seen them.

PETER: There are some BABES, dude! Like, some really hot girls. I was thinking we could, you know, shower, go up there, spit some game, talk up some girls, get some digits. Would you be down for that later?

ALLEN: Um...yeah, maybe.

PETER: Yeah, we can go by Commons later and--

ALLEN: Okay, Peter. I've been meaning to talk to you about something.

HALLMATE 2 (*enters, walks toward Allen and Peter, talking. NOTE: every year we did this skit the homophobic character was played by a female student who hammed up her over-the-top portrayal of this character as a means to demonstrate how ridiculous his attitudes were*). Yo—one more meeting, and I'm gonna die. I can't do it. Like, I CANNOT do it. All that sensitivity bullshit...like, I'm so over it. It's so gay. I just can't do it anymore. I'm so glad to meet you guys. You guys are my bros. I know we don't have any faggots on this hall—am I right?? Gonna be a good year! *(Slaps either Peter or Allen on the backside and exits).*

ALLEN: You know, I forgot. I told Catherine that I was going to study with her in...*(looks at watch)* right now.

PETER: Are you sure?

ALLEN: Yeah, we can meet up for dinner or something.

PETER: Okay! See you then!

(Each head off in different directions. ALLEN walks downstage to address the audience.)

ALLEN: I was planning to come out to my roommate at that point, but after that guy came by and made that really rude comment, I just...I couldn't come out then. I didn't feel comfortable or safe anymore, and I didn't know when I would feel comfortable again.

(ALLEN exits. PETER walks downstage to address the audience.)

PETER: At that moment, I really thought Allen was going to come out to me. And I'd really prepared myself for it. We'd become friends at this point, and I knew our friendship was too important for there to be secrets between us. But, after that guy acted like such a tool, I don't blame him for not opening up. I could still sense the tension between us, so after a few days, I decided to take matters into my own hands. I didn't know how it would end, but I was willing to take the risk.

(ALLEN and PETER's dorm room.)

PETER: Wanna play some FIFA?

ALLEN: Yeah, sure.

PETER: Oh, I was meaning to ask you. You've been hanging out with that Catherine girl a lot lately.

ALLEN: Mmhmm

PETER: She's hot, dude!

ALLEN: Yeah, she's cool.

PETER: Yeah, you tryin' to hit that up, or...?

ALLEN: No, we're just friends.

PETER: Oh...friend zone? That's rough, dude.

ALLEN: It's okay with me.

PETER: Alright. She got any other hot friends, though?

ALLEN: Ok, Peter. Listen. This is what I've been meaning to talk to you about. The thing is...I'm not really into girls.
PETER: You mean like the TV show?

ALLEN: No! I love the TV show. The TV show's great. But, seriously, Peter, I'm gay.

PETER: Well, I didn't wanna say anything, but I kinda felt like there was something you weren't telling me. And, I felt terrible to think that maybe I made you feel uncomfortable and couldn't talk to me about stuff. To be honest, I had my suspicions...and I didn't really know how I would handle it at first. But I'm glad you told me, man.

ALLEN: So...you're okay with it?

PETER: Yeah, man, you'll always be my bro. Who else is gonna kick my ass at FIFA all the time? And by the way, since you're just friends with that Catherine girl, you gotta hook me up with some digits!

ALLEN: Haha. We'll see.

Davidson College's original ending

(ALLEN comes downstage to address the audience.)
ALLEN: Hi, everyone. My name is Allen, and I am openly gay on campus. Actually, this skit was based on the experience I had with my freshman roommate. He made me feel really comfortable, and we even talked about these skits; how funny they were, and how he hoped anyone would feel comfortable coming out to their roommates at Davidson. I hope that if you are LGBTQ, you will feel comfortable

coming out and have the same positive experience I had. But, I know that can be a really difficult decision, and everyone's experience isn't mine. It was definitely the right decision for me. My advice would be to be yourself and trust your friends. And if you have questions or concerns, or want to talk to someone, there are lots of resources on campus to support you and help you figure things out.

Suggested ending for other performers

(ALLEN comes downstage to address the audience.)
ALLEN: Hi, everyone. This is the true story of a young man named Allen and his experience coming out to his college roommate. He agreed to share his story and have ACTORs dramatize it because he knew it could be a powerful tool to reassure other LGBTQ young people that even if they have experienced discrimination and intolerance in the past, this doesn't mean they will continue to experience that in the future. Allen was fortunate that he went to a college that tries very hard to be an inclusive community, but Allen also knew that even in accepting, diverse institutions there are still homophobic tools. He took a chance, was honest with his roommate and it strengthened their friendship. His advice to others is to be yourself and trust your friends – and find resources in your community that help and support you as you deal with this challenging time in your life – you definitely don't have to deal with coming out alone. [*Include references here to local resources available to LGBTQ youth*]

The Wild Thing
by Zabet NeuCollins
Loosely based on "Where the Wild Things Are" by Maurice Sendak and a keynote address by Jeff Levy

CHARACATERS in order of appearance:

ACTOR: A youth (MAX) who identifies as gay. Dresses in black clothing, nothing that would signify he is anything other than what he says he is.

BEASTS: Each is dressed in black, but has a devilish mask and has his/her "name" written clearly on the forehead or in some visible manner. The following descriptions are taken from Jeff Levy's address:

1 –STIGMA: *Stigma is the largest BEAST of all, and the one that labels Max as flawed.*

2 –SHAME: *Shame is a BEAST related to Stigma – in fact, they are twins. Shame follows Stigma wherever he goes. Shame surrounds Max and grows so thick and heavy that Max feels trapped. He can no longer see any of his inherent goodness. Instead, he sees only that he is bad.*

3 – JUDGMENT: *Judgment is a wild thing who is sometimes quite confusing. One of the older BEASTS, judgment hides behind a façade of wisdom, berating the other BEASTS with pseudo-knowledge based only on his own limited experience. Judgment is subtle, but his pushes and shoves leave Max imbalanced and uncertain of his path.*

4 – HARASSMENT: *Harassment is a cousin of judgment and much less subtle. Harassment takes over where judgment leaves off. Harassment is overt, domineering, mean, and abusive. On a good day, harassment only roars at Max, gnashes his teeth, and scares him with his yellow eyes. On a bad day, harassment hits Max, bites him, and kicks Max.*

5 - HOMOPHOBIA: *Homophobia is the daughter of Heterosexism. She pretends she is scared of Max and that somehow Max will hurt her. She whispers to the other wild things about Max's evil ways; how there is something about Max that will infect the other wild things. Homophobia breeds hatred. Ultimately, she makes Max hate himself.*

6 - HETEROSEXISM: *Heterosexism is one of the more sophisticated of the wild things. He focuses on giving rewards only to other wild things. Heterosexism acts like the wild things are the only ones who matter and treats Max like a second-class citizen in the forest. He instills in Max a belief that he doesn't deserve what the other creatures receive; that Max is not entitled to happiness, and that he is doomed to be somehow "less than everyone else" for the rest of his life.*

7 - REJECTION: *Rejection teases Max. She and her friends tease Max into thinking he has a chance for friendship and happiness, but then abandon him.*

8 - OSTRACISM: *Ostracism singles Max out from his place in the forest. Just when Max thinks he may have a friend in one of the wild things, Ostracism makes fun of Max, calls him names, and summons Shame and Stigma to help him berate and belittle Max. Ostracism likes to point out Max's faults, accentuating all the ways Max is different.*

9 - EXPLOITATION: *Exploitation is one of the sneakiest but most powerful of the wild things. He waits for Max to be at his most vulnerable. When Max is most in need of a friendly BEAST in the forest, Exploitation uses Max to do what he wants, and Max acquiesces because he is so lonely. Instead of being Max's friend, however, Exploitation exposes Max to circumstances he doesn't understand and from which he can't protect himself.*

10 - OPPRESSION: *Oppression, though he doesn't admit it openly, is the King of all the wild things. All the BEASTS follow his commands and all that happens to Max in his journey through the forest leads him to his meeting with Oppression. Oppression uses the other wild things: Stigma, Shame, Judgment, Harassment, Ostracism, Rejection, Heterosexism, Homophobia and Exploitation as a gang; a hugely powerful gang of wild things that traps Max, and strips him of his rights, his power, his ability to protect himself. Oppression is the ringleader and, as long as Oppression reigns, Max will forever be helpless.*

ACTOR enters stage. The BEASTS are standing behind him in a semi-circle. They are either turned around or they have their heads bowed. They do not move until it is their scene.

ACTOR: I knew from a young age that I was "different." And you know, when you're seven or so, being different means being bad. At that time, I definitely couldn't explain what exactly about me was different, but people still noticed. First my friends, and then my parents. My parents didn't take it that well — they don't do well under pressure — and they soon began referring to me when they thought I wasn't there as

BEASTS *(in unison)*: The Wild Thing.

ACTOR: One time when I was quite young, I told my parents at the dinner table about a new game my friend and I had come up with. I forget the details, but I know it involved wearing my mother's makeup and her dinner gown. Well, you should've seen my dad... *(laughs weakly)*

BEAST 1--STIGMA: WILD THING! TO BED WITH NO SUPPER!

(ACTOR goes to a bed, or a representation of a bed, and gets ready to go to sleep, miming everything. He rubs his stomach, hungry. He leans back in the bed, closes his eyes. As he does this, the BEASTS start to creep up around him, whispering and getting louder with each repetition).

BEASTS *(in unison)*: Wild thing, wild thing, wild thing, wild thing, WILD THING!

ACTOR *(sits up)*: AH!

(The BEASTS scatter.)

ACTOR: Hello? Is... is anyone there?

(BEAST 1 & 2 --STIGMA & SHAME emerge from the darkness. They peer at him, and the ACTOR shrinks in his bed.)

ACTOR: Who are you?

BEAST 1: I think we should be asking —

BEAST 2: Who are you?

ACTOR: I'm Max.

BEAST 1: No, no, no. We didn't mean your name. We meant—
BEAST 2: *What* are you?

ACTOR: I'm—I'm a boy—

BEAST 1: But you're not like other little boys, are you?

BEAST 2: You smell… different.
ACTOR: Different?

BEAST 1 (*guffaws*): He doesn't smell different, he is different! And you know what we think of different boys?

ACTOR: Wh—what?

BEAST 1: We think you're rather tasty. Oh, yes, so tasty.

ACTOR: You want to eat me?

BEAST 2: No, Max, you want us to eat you. Because that would be the best thing for everyone. You think your parents want to take care of you, day in and day out? They call you…

All BEASTS (*in unison*): The Wild Thing.

BEAST 2: Do you think you friends want to hang out with you? No, Max, you're different. And no one…

BEAST 1: No one

BEAST 2: Likes a boy who's different.

ACTOR: Go away!

(BEAST 3--JUDGEMENT enters.)

BEAST 3: You heard the boy, go away.

(BEAST 1 & 2 give him dirty looks and leave. BEAST 3 pulls up a stool and sits on it. He looks at Max for a while.)

BEAST 3: So.

ACTOR: Who are you?

BEAST 3: That doesn't matter. Who are you?
ACTOR: I'm Max.

BEAST 3 *(highly judgmental)*: Hm.

ACTOR: Do you ... do you think I am different?

BEAST 3: I don't think that's the question you should be asking.

ACTOR: What do you mean?

BEAST 3: The fact is Max, you are different. You can tell.

ACTOR: You can?

BEAST 3: Of course you can! Everyone can. It's in your mannerisms, the way you speak, the way you dress, the way you move. Everyone can see a mile away that you are different.

(ACTOR looks confused.)

BEAST 3: So do you know the question yet?

ACTOR: The question?

BEAST 3: C'mon boy, stick with me. The question you should be asking.

ACTOR: I... I don't know.

BEAST 3: The question is, "What are you going to do?"

ACTOR: Do I need to do anything?

BEAST 3: Do you need to do anything? Hah! Good joke.

ACTOR: It wasn't.

BEAST 3: It wasn't what?

ACTOR *(whispers)*: It wasn't a joke.

BEAST 3 *(raises eyebrows and leans back, highly judgmental)*: Ah.

(BEAST 4--HARASSMENT and 5--HOMOPHOBIA enter. 4 is looking at ACTOR like he is a delicious treat, but 5 looks repulsed and scared. ACTOR doesn't notice them until 4 jumps and tackles ACTOR on his bed. ACTOR screams and squirms away, escaping to the edge of his bed.)

BEAST 5 *(screams)*: Get away from him! He'll infect you!

BEAST 4 *(ignoring her)*: So, Max, what are you going to do?

BEAST 3: Oh, get out of here you two.

BEAST 4: Noooo, you already had your turn. It's my turn. He looks so tasty. I just want to eat him up.

ACTOR & BEAST 5: No!

BEAST 5: You'll get infected!

BEAST 4 *(ignoring her, focusing on ACTOR)*: You think you can tell me what to do? You, with your different ways? Your different smell? Your different hair? Your different clothes? You think you can tell me what to do?

ACTOR: I—I didn't mean—

BEAST 4: Then you'd better watch what you're saying, little freak, because   otherwise—

(BEAST 4 edges towards ACTPR, licking his lips. ACTOR starts to panic.)

ACTOR: No—no—

BEAST 5: Get away! He's going to infect you! He's different!

ACTOR: No—no—

(BEAST 6--HETEROSEXISM enters. He sees ACTOR.)

BEAST 6: Oh yay, yippee! A boy! Another boy! Come here, 4, stop scaring him.

(BEAST 4 reluctantly lets ACTOR go. BEAST 6 gets a good look at him.)

BEAST 6: Now let's see here, a little boy. Let's look at you. Oh—you're not—

(He turns to go.)

ACTOR: Wait! I'm not what?

BEAST 6: You're not a normal little boy. If you were a normal little boy, I would've taken you to the festival. We've had a bunch lately; it's been perfect. A lot of little boys running away from home-- we snatch them up and take them to the festival. It's just jolly good fun— The Wild Rumpus, we call it. But occasionally… well, occasionally we'll catch a boy like you, and it's just too bad, such a disgrace.

ACTOR: There are others like me?

BEAST 6: Once in a blue moon. No, no, no, I'm sorry, but I just can't let you come with me to the festival. You see, it wouldn't be fair. If all the normal little boys saw me bring in you, they would throw a fit! And they would begin to question-- what does it even mean to be normal? They would lose their sense of identity, you know, and I couldn't have that. No, no, it's better this way. You just remain in this bed and we'll come get you when the festival is over.

ACTOR: I just want to go home.

BEAST 6: Well good luck with that. Come on guys, the Wild Rumpus is about the start. Look smart!

(3 & 4 stand up, 5 cowering behind them.)

ACTOR: Ex—excuse me?

BEAST 6: Yes?

ACTOR: How—how do I get home?

(All the BEASTS laugh.)

BEAST 6: I don't think I've ever met a little boy who has made it home on his own, let alone a little boy like you.

BEAST 4: You don't know what is lurking behind the trees, little Maxie boy. Maybe a ghost, or a hungry monster, or… worst of all… another boy like you.

(BEAST 5 screams.)

BEAST 6: Come on, let's go.

BEAST 4: Bye, freak.

(BEASTS exit. ACTOR is left by himself, and he is pretty frightened.)

ACTOR: Hello? Is anyone out there? Mom? Dad?

(BEAST 7--REJECTION enters. She is pretty curious.)

BEAST 7: And what do we have here?
ACTOR: No! I don't want to meet you! Go away!

BEAST 7: You don't want to meet me? But why not?

ACTOR: You're mean!

BEAST 7: Now that's a nasty thing to say. You haven't even met me.

ACTOR: I don't care!

BEAST 7: I think you need to loosen up, kiddo. I just want to have fun. We all just want to have fun.

(BEASTS 1 & 2 enter, followed by 8--OSTRACISM. ACTOR sees them and his eyes widen.)

ACTOR: No! I don't like you! Go away!

BEAST 8: Would you look at that. Just a sniveling little cry baby.

BEAST 7: C'mon, Maxie, all we want to do is have fun.

ACTOR: Fun?

BEAST 7: Yeah. Do you want to play ball?

ACTOR: I don't—I don't have a ball.

BEAST 7: That's why we brought one.

(She motions to 1 and they procure a ball.)

BEAST 8: I bet he couldn't even catch a ball if he tried.

ACTOR: I—I can. I play baseball.

BEAST 2: You lie. Boys like you don't play baseball.

BEAST 8: You play with dolls, don't you?

BEAST 1: Anyhow, this isn't baseball. This is monster ball.

BEAST 7: Do you want to play with us, little Maxie?

ACTOR: I—I guess.

(BEAST 7 passes the ball to the other monsters. They pass it back and forth for a long time, ignoring ACTOR. Gradually they maneuver so ACTOR is in the middle, jumping on his bed, trying to catch the ball.)

ACTOR: Pass to me! Hey, I'm open!

(BEAST 7 throws the ball and it hits ACTOR in the stomach. He flops over, his breath knocked out of him. All the BEASTS burst out laughing, and they take off. ACTOR is left with the ball and he looks dejected. He begins to cry.)

ACTOR: I just want to go home.

(BEAST 9--EXPLOITATION enters.)

BEAST 9: Oh, you poor, poor boy.

ACTOR: Wh—who are you?

BEAST 9: I'm your friend. *(He sits on ACTOR'S bed)*

ACTOR: I don't have any friends. And plus, you're one of them.

BEAST 9: Are you calling me a monster? Oh, that's hurts.

ACTOR: You look like one.

BEAST 9: That hurts, Maxie boy. Didn't your mother teach you anything? Not to call people names?

ACTOR *(ashamed)*: I'm sorry.

BEAST 9: Oh, it's okay. I understand. Anyhow, now that I'm here, well, I thought we might be able to do something.

ACTOR: Do something?

BEAST 9: Yes, you see, there's sort of this festival going on.

ACTOR: The Wild Rumpus!

BEAST 9: That's the one! And anyhow, I was wondering if you wanted to go.

ACTOR: But—one of the monsters told me I couldn't go.

BEAST 9: He just meant to the gathering of little boys. I want to take you   somewhere else.
ACTOR: Where?

BEAST 9: At the end of the festival, there's this BIG feast. Everyone gathers, the most important monsters of all time, and we all eat and have a lot of fun. Anyhow, we're supposed to come with a friend, and I didn't have anyone, and I thought if maybe you put on this *(pulls out a miniature monster mask)*, you could come with me.

ACTOR: I don't know…

BEAST 9: Come on. Are you going to let your only friend down? Put on the mask, and you'll see.

(ACTOR hesitatingly puts on the mask.)

BEAST 9: Ah! Would you look at that! A miniature monster. Perfect.

ACTOR *(eager)*: I look like a monster?

BEAST 9: A perfect replica. Now what do you say, little Maxie? Will you help a friend out?

(ACTOR pauses for a long time.)

ACTOR: I guess I can help.

BEAST 9: Yippee! We're going to have so much fun, Max, you'll see.

(He grabs ACTORS hand and they walk, walk, and walk. Finally, they walk in on a group of monsters. Immediately, 9 rips off ACTOR'S mask.)

BEAST 9: I have him! Look, 10, I have him!

ACTOR: No!

(He tries to run, but 9 catches him and holds him tight. BEAST 10--OPPRESSION slowly turns around. 10 is the biggest, most insidious, and most powerful of all wild things. He looks at ACTOR.)

BEAST 10: Well, well, well. What do we have here?

ACTOR: Go away! Go away!

BEAST 10: A little boy. And he's *(pauses dramatically)* different.

(BEAST 10 slowly advances. All the other BEASTS follow him, smacking their lips.)

BEASTS *(in unison)*: Wild thing, wild thing, wild thing, wild thing.

BEAST 10: You're a wild thing, Maxie. And I think I want to eat you up.

(The BEASTS surround him. There is no escape for ACTOR, and out of desperation, ACTOR tries to attack. He hits, kicks, spits in the faces of the wild things that have joined Oppression. With mock outrage, they laugh at ACTOR and grab him, trapping him further.)

ACTOR: Noooo! NOOOOOO! Let me go!

BEAST 10: And why would we let you go, Max?

ACTOR: I'm just a boy!

BEASTS (in unison): WRONG!

BEAST 10: Wrong, Max. You're not just a little boy. You're different. And difference means – we get to eat you up. One little finger by one little finger, one arm, then the other. Bit by bit, we will tear you apart until there is-

BEASTS (in unison): NOTHING

BEAST 10: Left.

(The BEASTS all start grabbing at parts of him, snapping their jaws.)

ACTOR: No, no, no! BE STILL!

(All the BEASTS freeze. ACTOR untangles himself from the mess. He goes to the center of stage.)

ACTOR: There are a lot of little kids like me. Those who journey into the forest where the wild things are. Sometimes we make it home. (He pauses and looks at all the BEASTS) Sometimes, we don't.

Four times more likely to be threatened with a weapon;
Three times more likely to drop out of school;
Four times more likely to be sexually abused and more likely not to report it;
Three times more likely to attempt suicide;

The wild things are here. They are all around us. Lurking in the forests or in the streets, the hallways or the cafeterias: it doesn't matter where. Wherever they are, their power is pervasive. They will tear those who are vulnerable apart.

Did you know that these monsters have such power? Did you know that they could do this to me, to kids just like me? Did you know such wild things exist?

(Pause)

Did you know you may be one of those wild things?

(ACTOR looks over audience. He puts his wild mask back on and joins the monsters who have resumed a semi-circle behind him. They march out silently, one by one.)

END

Excerpt from "Where the Wild Things Are: Enhancing Resilience in LGBTQ Youth"
by Jeff Levy

Wild things live among us. They work with us, eat with us, share drinks with us, socialize with us, befriends us… Sometimes, both knowingly and unknowingly, we encourage them. How do you confront these wild things without making young people like Max more vulnerable in the process?

Regardless of who you are and where you come from, your goal is to strengthen all young people, not to oppress or disempower them. How do you strengthen character, foster mental health, build self-confidence, and enhance resiliency in LGBTQ youth? The challenge is to hold your own values and honor your own morality, while at the same time, to not engage in any behavior that hurts or confuses young people like Max. How can you do this?

Engage in affirmative practice with LGBTQ youth. What does this mean? Gay affirmative practice means you SEE the wild things. You know that whoever Max is, whomever he loves, the problems he experiences do not reside in him. They are a result of all of the effects of the wild things. Max's sadness, depression, isolation, his substance use, his truancy, even his offensive behavior toward others, are all symptoms of being oppressed. The goal of affirmative practice is to help Max feel better about himself and to diminish the harm caused by each and every one of the wild things. When possible, affirmative practice seeks to identify and rid the world of wild things altogether; to make the forest a safer place for all young people.

Open yourself to the possibility that ANY child might be LGBTQ. Do not assume all youth and families are heterosexual. Do not assume that you will be able to identify with all LGBTQ youth and families, or that they will openly disclose their sexual orientation or gender identity to you, even if you come right out and ask. Some young people may not be able to accept their orientation and may still be struggling with their feelings. Not all LGBTQ youth and families are gender non-conforming or identifiable by the stereotypes which are most commonly associated with LGBTQ youth and families.

Always assure youth that it is okay to be LGBTQ; that it is okay to be confused; that it is okay not to get involved or enter into a relationship; that it is okay to go back and forth and change his/her mind. If it helps, refer youth and families to non-sexual, healthy peer support groups within their local communities or schools. Social interaction between other LGBTQ youth and families will help to alleviate the extreme social isolation and loneliness which most LGBTQ youth and families experience. Help other people to view homosexuality from a non-judgmental, non-pejorative perspective; to understand the impact of stigma and stigma management on identity integration. Help others assess and address the effects of homophobia and oppression on LGBTQ youth rather than focus on being LGBTQ as the problem.

The most important thing is to emphasize good care for all children regardless of race, culture, physical abilities, religion, or sexual orientation. This is not just about improving care for LGBTQ youth. If the wild things are out there, they're biting EVERYONE who is, in some way different or vulnerable. They attack all young people who in some way do not fit what the majority considers normal. Wild things attack LGBTQ youth, but they also attack youth of color, youth with disabilities, youth who are overweight, youth who are shy, youth who are Muslim, youth who are Jewish, and the list of vulnerable young people goes on. There many young people who are dealing with the effects of the wild things and may not be managing them very well, and they need our help.

Consider your options. Will you be a wild thing? Or will you accept everyone as who they are, regardless of race, creed, and sexual orientation? Will you be an advocate for inclusion?

Seek not, my soul, the life of the immortals; but enjoy to the full the resources that are within thy reach.
- Pindar

Resources

Major Contributors to Out & Allied Volume 2

Dreams of Hope
Out & Allied Vol. 2 is pleased and grateful to have permission to reprint a number of pieces from Dreams of Hope (DOH), a Pittsburgh, PA based arts organization which has been providing creative outlets and positive role models and messages for LGBTQ and allied youth since 2003. DOH provides LGBTQ youth a welcoming environment to grow in confidence, express themselves, and develop as leaders. The DOH songs, poems, and skits were written by youth (ages 13-21) in collaboration with local artists to convey the youth's own experiences. The collected materials from DOH's first 10 years have been anthologized and can be purchased at: dreamsofhope.org/anthology

The New Conservatory Theatre Center:
YouthAware Out & United (Y.O.U.)
For over 30 years Ed Decker, the Founding Artistic Director has been working to provide the San Francisco community with high quality youth education programming, Queer & Allied theatre, children's theatre, and new play development with emerging artists' residencies to support local and national artists. For over two decades, NCTC's YouthAware Educational Theatre program has produced plays for young people that entertain, illuminate social issues, inspire and encourage healthier life choices.

[Un]spoken Maine
A Man Defined; Grampy; The Rules; and Him, Her & Me, were created as a result of collaboration between the theatre department and campus safety project at the University of Southern Maine, under direction of Meghan Brodie with some consultation by Add Verb. [Un]spoken Maine is a project consisting of student-written and student-performed pieces about sexual health, safety, and communication. [Un]Spoken Maine has helped foster student and community conversations around shaping safe, healthy relationships and offering support to those who might be struggling to escape abusive ones.

The Waterville Inclusive Community Project (WICP)
Founded in 2013, WICP brings together organizations and individuals who are invested in creating welcoming and safe spaces for LGBTQ youth in Waterville, Maine and neighboring communities. The WICP works to empower Lesbian, Gay, Bisexual, Trans, Queer, and Questioning (LGBTQ) youth and their allies to be leaders and change agents in their schools and communities.

LGBTQ & ALLIED PLACES, SPACES & FACES

Pride Youth Theater Alliance (PYTA)

PYTA connects and supports queer youth theater organizations, programs, and professionals committed to empowering lesbian, gay, bisexual, transgender, queer and allied (LGBTQA) youth in North America: www.prideyouththeateralliance.org

PYTA Member Organizations

About Face Theater

About Face is an identity affirming theatre activism program based at Chicago, Il.

www.aboutfacetheatre.com

Add Verb Productions/University of New England

Out & Allied is a youth writing project which uses the power of performance to communicate and educate.

www.addverbproductions.org/programs/outallied

Buddies in Bad Times Theatre: Queer Youth Arts Program

Buddies in Bad Times Theatre creates theatre by developing and presenting voices that question sexual and cultural norms. Built on the political and social principles of queer liberation, Buddies supports artists and works that reflect and advance these values.

buddiesinbadtimes.com/youth

Creative Action: Outside the Lines Youth Theatre Ensemble

Outside the Lines is part of a Creative Action partnership with Out Youth and the University of Texas Department of Theatre and Dance. Out Youth's mission is to promote the physical, mental, emotional, spiritual and social well being of sexual and gender minority youth so that they can openly and safely explore and affirm their identities.

creativeaction.org/programs/youth-ensembles

Dreams of Hope
Formed in 2003 to develop LGBTQ youth leaders who educate audiences about issues they face, each performance includes a youth led discussion.
> www.dreamsofhope.org/programs

Fringe Benefits
Fringe Benefits is a groundbreaking educational theatre company whose workshops and productions have earned the commendations of youth, educators, parents and community leaders.
> www.cootieshots.org/

Gay and Lesbian Service Organization (GSO): Company Q
Company Q is a unique performance/ social justice theatre troupe for young people focusing on queer issues. It is based at the Gay and Lesbian Service Organization in Lexington, Kentucky.
> www.facebook.com/companyqlexington

Lifeworks, LA Gay & Lesbian Center: Outset Theater
LifeWorks and Outfest, two independent non-profit organizations working together nurtures and inspires aspiring young filmmakers. OutSet provides participants with access to and guidance by working professional mentors from the film and television industries.
> lifeworksla.org/outset/index.html

The Neutral Zone: Riot Youth
Riot Youth, a program for LGBTQ teens operates out of The Neutral Zone in Ann Arbor, Michigan. Through leadership skill building, community organizing, networking, and socializing, Riot Youth connects youth to build an inclusive community. Teens also engage in social justice through theater, dialogue, lobbying and other advocacy efforts.
> www.neutral-zone.org

The New Conservatory Theatre Center:
YouthAware Out & United (Y.O.U.)
Y.O.U. provides LGBTQI teens and their allies an empowered voice though theater, as well as provide a safe and welcoming venue for sharing their stories, triumphs, and concerns about being a lesbian, gay, bi-sexual, transgender, questioning, or straight allied teen in the Bay Area.
> www.nctcsf.org/you.htm

New Orleans Queer Youth Theater Project

The New Orleans Queer Youth Theater is a space where youth can explore varied and fluid performances of queerness, harness their voice and power through theater making techniques, and hang out with other queer and allied youth.

> www.facebook.com/pages/New-Orleans-
> Queer-Youth-Theater/145327728986491

Oakland Center for the Arts: YOUnify Theatre Company

Developed through a Mukti Fund grant, YOUnify provides the place for all Queer Youth of the Mahoning Valley to tell their stories through theatre, music and art.

> oaklandcenter.com

Omaha Theater Company at the Rose: Pride Players

Pride Players uses improvisation to create songs, poetry, monologues, and skits that explore what it means to be a gay, lesbian, bisexual, transgendered, or straight-allied teen in Omaha.

> www.rosetheater.org/classes-programs/
> 2013-14-teen-season/pride-players-project-15

Proud Theater

Proud Theater is open to 13-19 year-old LGBTQ youth, children of LGBTQ parents, or allies of the LGBTQ community. This innovate theatre program allows the youth to tell their own stories and is designed to foster self-expression and self-empowerment for youth around the state of Wisconsin.

> www.proudtheater.org

Rainbow Pride Youth Alliance: FIERCE (RPYA)

PRYA provides a safe, healthy, and enriching environment for LGBTQI youth in Ontario, Riverside, and San Bernardino in Southern California. RPYA is a safe haven where youth are supported and challenged to engage fully in their own personal, social, and artistic development. FIERCE is a peer-led wellness strategy designed to introduce youth and their families to the power of art, enhancing communication across generations and building a stronger community and neighborhood. Theater is used as a tool for enhancing self-esteem, developing language and communication skills, strengthening cultural identity, increasing academic and vocational skill sets, and promoting literacy.

> www.rpya-ie.org

The Coterie Theatre: Project Pride
LGBTQ and straight allied teens creates theatre that gives voice to their experiences, culminating in a production that challenges the assumptions and celebrates the diversity of the participants and audience. Project Pride is guided by: Love, Generosity, Beauty, Truth.
> thecoterie.org

The Queer Youth Theater at The Door (QYT)
Based in New York City, The Queer Youth Theater creates original pieces using the ideas and concerns of young people in the group. QYT meets at The Door, a comprehensive youth services organization in Manhattan. The group is primarily intended for LGBTQIA youth, but includes straight allies.
> www.facebook.com/pages/
> The-Queer-Youth-Theater/244446522294077

The GLBT Community Center of Colorado:
Rainbow Alley Theater Program
This program teaches youth to perform scripted and self-scripted theatrical works for the greater community. The philosophy of the program is to support youth in the development of amplifying their voice and refining their craft, while addressing the serious issues that LGBTQ youth face, including bullying, rejection by families, homelessness, discrimination, violence, depression, and suicide.
> www.glbtcolorado.org/rainbow-alley/
> rainbow-alley-programs-and-services

The Theater Offensive: True Colors: Out Youth Theater
Provides year-round theater programming for lesbian, gay, bisexual, transgender, queer and questioning youth and their straight allies (LGBTQQA), ages 14 to 22. Dedicated to presenting an honest portrayal of the lives of LGBTQQA youth through group playwriting, production, performance and theater training intensives.
> www.thetheateroffensive.org/?page_id=2970

Theater Askew Youth Performance Experience (TAYPE)
An educational theatre program that empowers lesbian, gay, bisexual, transgender, and questioning (LGBTQ) youth and their allies in the New York area by nurturing and developing their unique theatrical voices.
> www.theatreaskew.com/taype.htm

Theatre UCF and Zebra Coalition: interACTionZ

An all-inclusive youth theatre partnership between Orlando Repertory Theatre, Theatre UCF, and the Zebra Coalition in Orlando, Florida. This hands-on and thought-provoking program is designed for LGBTQ+ youth and youth who identify as straight advocates for the LGBTQ+ community. interACTionZ focuses on using theatre for social change techniques in order to build community, creatively explore conflict-resolution, and develop youth leadership skills.

> facebook.com/interACTionZ

Waterville Inclusive Community Project: Out & Allied Youth Theatre

Established through Mukti's Queer Youth Theater Incubator Fund, a core of LGBTQ youth and their allies will perform, direct and write original performance pieces to create change in their schools and communities.

> wicpme.wordpress.com/2013/07/06/
> pride-youth-theater-alliance-grant/

Camps

This is not a comprehensive list and includes only camps located in the United States.

Camp Hawkeye (NH)

The mission at Camp Hawkeye is to bring together a diverse community of individuals that include campers, aged 8-16, and staff from a variety of geographic, socioeconomic, cultural, ethnic, and religious backgrounds.

> 781-315-1297
> 617-960-6740
> www.camphawkeye.com

Camp Highlight (NY)

Overnight camp for youth aged 8-15 who have a lesbian, gay, bisexual or transgender parent.

> 646-535-2267
> camphighlight.com/wp

Camp It Up! (CA)

Camp It Up is known for one-of-a-kind gay family vacations. They respect and celebrate all unique families and welcome you to find out more and join them this summer.

> www.campitup.org

Camp Lightbulb (MA)
Overnight summer camp for LGBT youth aged 14-18 in Province-town. Four different sessions to pick from.
> 508-237-7651
> www.camplightbulb.org/p/camp.html

CampOUT (MA)
CampOUT at Open View Farm is a unique farm/camp where young people from LGBTQ families are productive members of the farm community and share in the fun of summer camp activities. It is a place where difference and diversity are celebrated and children can be themselves. Young people have the opportunity to talk openly about their families and their experiences of LGBTQ familes.
> 413-369-0240.
> www.openviewfarm.org/campout

Camp OUTdoors! (AZ)
OUTdoors! Camp is dedicated to helping Lesbian, Gay, Bisexual, Transgender, and Queer youth develop leadership skills, work in collaborative ways, and develop a strong sense of self and community.
> 602-909-9956
> kado@onenten.org
> outdoorsgaycamp.com

CampOut Maine (ME)
CampOUT is a social and educational retreat for Lesbian, Gay, Bisexual, Transgender, Queer, Questioning, and Allied youth 14 - 22 years old. It is a space designed for young people to connect, learn, and share ideas. CampOUT empowers youth to explore issues of social justice and develop strong community.
> 207-200-GLBT
> campoutmaine@gmail.com
> www.campoutmaine.com

Camp Outright and Common Ground Center (VT)
Camp Outright is a six day/five night residential summer camp program for LGBTQQA youth, ages thirteen and older, from throughout U.S.A. The program will be a traditional summer camp experience and campers will participate in a wide variety of daily activities based upon their interests, as well as special topical work-shops to address needs stated by LGBTQQA youth.
> 1-800-430-2667
> www.campoutright.org

Camp Ten Trees (WA)

Camp Ten Trees is a nonprofit organization offering summer camp sessions in the Pacific Northwest, featuring a week for lesbian, gay, bisexual, transgender, queer, questioning, and allied (LGBTQA) youth, and a week for children and youth of LGBTQ and/or non-traditional families.

> 206-288-9568
> info@camptentrees.org
> www.camptentrees.org

Pushing Margins (CA)

Pushing Margins is an organization designed to empower LGBTQQIAA youth from across the Bay Area through arts education. The annual summer camp and workshops bring youth together to paint, draw, write, and otherwise create a new youth art culture.

> info@pushingmargins.org
> pushingmargins.org/camp

Summer Qamp (WV)

Dreams of Hope hosts an overnight arts camp every summer at the Emma Kaufmann Camp near Morgantown, West Virginia, for LGBTQ youth ages 13-19. Each camp day include arts, games, educational workshops, and traditional camp activities.

> 412-361-2065
> www.dreamsofhope.org/camp

The following camps are not specifically directed toward LGBTQ youth and families but they put special emphasis on inclusivity, all types of diversity, and social justice. Again, this list is not exhaustive and only covers the United States.

Camp Celo (NC)

Camp Celo is born out of the Quaker values of non-violence, simplicity, and environmental awareness. The central belief is that the Light of God exists in each person. There is a spiritual element to life at camp that focuses on the universal principles of compassion, cooperation, integrity, responsibility, and service common to all major religions. The program stresses cooperation and minimizes competition and regimentation.

> 828-675-4323
> www.campcelo.com

Camp Nashoba North (ME)
Camp Nashoba creates an atmosphere that enables our campers to make good decisions and fosters personal growth through the achievement of goals and supportive community living. They want their campers to develop an appreciation and sense of stewardship towards the environment and the outdoors.

    207-655-7170

    campnashoba.com

Camp Onas Quaker Camp (PA)
The Quaker camp for all kids, ages 8 to 13! Camp Onas strives to create a fun environment and a feeling of community among our campers that lasts for years

    610-847-5858

    www.camponas.org

Circle Pines Center (MI)
The mission of Circle Pines is to teach peace, social justice, environmental stewardship and cooperation. The Center aims to demonstrate cooperative alternatives for economic and social issues and to teach cooperation as a way of life.

    269-623-5555

    www.circlepinescenter.org

Summer Fenn (MA)
Summer Fenn is committed to guiding and celebrating our campers as they make choices about how to participate in our many programs. They challenge each camper to take responsibility for his or her own actions and attitudes, making the experience a positive one for everyone. The Summer Fenn Way is about seeking out ways to treat each other well and helping to make someone else's day better.

    978-318-3614

    www.fenn.org/podium/default.aspx?t=130002

Conferences and Retreats

LGBT Leadership Institute
A five-month learning experience centered on a three-day training with many online elements.
> www.anderson.ucla.edu/executive-education/
> individual-executives/leadership-suite/
> lgbt-leadership-institute

The LGBTQ Muslim Retreat
Weekend retreat for self-reflection and community building. During the weekend you will engage in workshops, interactive sessions, salaat (prayer), creative writing, zikr (remembrance), art, reflections from the Quran and the Prophet's life, poetry, song, and muraqabah (silent meditation).
> www.lgbtmuslimretreat.com

The National Conference on LGBT Equality: Creating Change
The conference is run by the National Gay and Lesbian Task Force, and attracts more than 3,500 people from all over the country every year. Presenters and participants come from all walks of life and include members of the business community, elected officials, students, faith leaders and staff and volunteers of non-profit organizations.
> www.creatingchange.org

Human Rights Campaign: Time to Thrive
An annual national conference promoting safety, inclusion and well-being for LGBTQ youth.
> timetothrive.org

Youth Toolkits

Gayrilla: A Tool Kit for LGBTQ Youth

Gayrilla seeks to create change in school communities through participatory evaluation, theatre performances, and educational dialogues.

> http://neutral-zone.org

Stand Up Action Kit: By Maya Brown and Treva deMaynadier

Created in Partnership with the Waterville Inclusive Community Partnership. This toolkit provides performance pieces, activities, and resources designed to help you organize trainings and other events in your community focused around creating a more accepting community for LGBTQ youth.

> http://wicpme.wordpress.com/2013/08/29/
> a-summer-project-to-aid-the-nation

Religious Resources

Affirmation: Gay and Lesbian Mormons

Affirmation's membership consists of individuals at different stages in the coming-out process, as well as families, friends and allies. Their mission is to provide a safe space where LGBTQ individuals, as well as those questioning their orientation, can associate with like individuals, ask questions, and know that they are not alone. Affirmation helps LGBTQ people reconcile with their spirituality within the context of a common Mormon background.

> www.affirmation.org

Association of Welcoming and Affirming Baptists (AWAB)

The mission of the AWAB is to create and support a community of churches, organizations and individuals committed to the inclusion of gay, lesbian, bisexual and transgender persons in the full life and mission of Baptist churches.

> www.awab.org

Eshel: Creating an LGBT-inclusive Orthodox world

Eshel works to create community and acceptance for lesbian, gay, bisexual, and transgender Jews and their families in Orthodox communities.

> www.eshelonline.org/

The Gay and Lesbian Vaishnava Association (GALVA)
GALVA's purpose is to educate Vaishnavas, Hindus and the public in general about the "third sex" as described in Vedic literatures to help correct many of the common misconceptions people hold today concerning third-gender people (gays, lesbians, bisexuals, transgenders, the intersexed, etc.). GALVA also wishes to provide a friendly and positive-oriented place where third-gender devotees and guests can associate together and utilize their time to learn more about Krsna consciousness and advance in spiritual life.
> www.galva108.org

Gay Buddhist Fellowship (GBF)
The Gay Buddhist Fellowship supports Buddhist practice in the Gay men's community. It is a forum that brings together the diverse Buddhist traditions to address the spiritual concerns of Gay men. GBF's mission includes cultivating a social environment that is inclusive and caring.
> www.gaybuddhist.org

Gay Christian Network (GCN)
Founded in 2001, the GCN is a nonprofit Christian ministry dedicated to building bridges and offering support for those caught in the crossfire of one of today's most divisive culture wars. GCN helps create safe spaces both online and offline for Christians of all sorts to make friends, ask questions, get support, and offer support to others.
> www.gaychristian.net

Human Rights Campaign (HRC)
Many helpful resources dedicated to working toward LGBT equal rights. This is the link to resources that are specifically focused on religion and faith:
> www.hrc.org/resources/category/religion-faith

This is a sampling of what they have to offer:
Living Openly in Your Place of Worship
> www.hrc.org/resources/entry/
> living-openly-in-your-place-of-worship

Faith Advocacy 101 Packet
> www.hrc.org/files/assets/resources/
> Faith_Advocacy_101_Packet.pdf

Faith in Action
> www.hrc.org/resources/entry/faith-in-action

Imaan

Imaan supports LGBTQ Muslim people, along with their families and friends, to address issues of sexual orientation within Islam. It provides a safe space and support network to address issues of common concern through sharing individual experiences and institutional resources. Imaan promotes the Islamic values of peace, social justice, and tolerance through their work, and aspires to bring about a world that is free from prejudice and discrimination against all Muslims and LGBTQ people.

> www.imaan.org.uk

Jewish Queer Youth: JQY: Supporting LGBT Jews and their Families in the Orthodox Community

JQY's mission is to address the unique needs of LGBTQ frum* and formerly frum Jews. JQY is dedicated to cultivating a Jewish community where no one feels alone, bullied or silenced because of their orientation or gender identity. Special attention is given to youth, young adults and their families; however, programs for all ages exist. JQY programming reflects the support, community building, awareness and advocacy needs of their community.
*Frum includes: "Orthodox, Yeshivish, Chasidish, Sephardic, modern, and traditional Jewish identities"

> www.jqyouth.org/index.shtml

Keshet Ga'avah: The World Congress of Gay, Lesbian, Bisexual, and Transgender Jews

The World Congress holds conferences and workshops representing the interests of lesbian, gay, bisexual, & transgender Jews around the world. The focus of these sessions varies from regional, national, continental, and global.

> glbtjews.org/

Muslims for Progressive Values (MPV)

MPV's mission is to embody and be an effective voice of the traditional Quranic ideals of human dignity, egalitarianism, compassion, and social justice. MPV asserts that Islam is inherently progressive, inclusive, and egalitarian; an understanding from which their community is built.

> mpvusa.org/

'My Mind Was Changed'

A Communications Toolkit: A New Way to Talk with Conflicted Christians about LGBT People in Church and Society by Auburn Media, Fenton and Goodwin Simon Strategic Research. Funded by the Arcus Foundation. This toolkit provides powerful approaches to moving conflicted Christians from standing against LGBTQ equality to standing for it, in both the church and state.

www.groundswell-movement.org/wp-content/
uploads/2012/04/My-Mind-Was-Changed.pdf

Nehirim

Nehirim is a national community of LGBTQ Jews, families, and allies, committed to a more just and inclusive world. Nehirim's retreats, student programs, and community events transform lives. They are a leading Jewish voice for equality on the national stage.

www.nehirim.org

Other Sheep

Other Sheep is a worldwide ecumenical Christian organization dedicated to empowering sexual minorities throughout the world with the Good News of God's unconditional love for all and salvation through God's Son, Jesus Christ.

www.othersheep.org

QueerDharma: A Community of Practice

Queer Dharma is a community of meditation practice for all people, founded and hosted by LGBTQ people in New York City. A broad range of Buddhist traditions are represented in their membership and visiting teachers. There are many levels of experience with meditation and dharma, from questioning/beginners to long-time practitioners. All people are warmly welcome.

www.queerdharma.org

Religious Coalition Against Discrimination (RCAD)

RCAD works to create a beloved community that affirms and welcomes LGBT and other marginalized people, and invites all to join in transforming congregations and communities toward this end. To implement this vision, RCAD educates to change hearts and minds; promotes LGBT safety, equality, and inclusion; and advocates for social justice in ways that make LGBT concerns visible.

www.rcadmaine.org/

The United Church of Christ Coalition (UCC) for LGBT Concerns
The Coalition provides support and sanctuary to all their LGBT sisters and brothers, their families and friends; advocates for their full inclusion in church and society; and brings Christ's affirming message of love and justice for all people.
     www.ucccoalition.org

Other Organizations

The organizations included below are only a handful of the ones that exist. Many of them have regional chapters, and there are many, many more regional and local organizations all over the country and the world. We hope that this list is encouraging, and shows just how much action and support is out there. Want to get involved with or know more about an organization? Visit their website, or better yet give them a call!

For Colored Boys Who Have Considered Suicide When The Rainbow Is Still Not Enough: 4 Colored Boys
4 Colored Boys addresses longstanding issues of sexual abuse, suicide, HIV/AIDS, racism, and homophobia in the African American and Latino communities, and more specifically among young gay men of color.
     4coloredboys.com

Alcohol Addiction Helpline
Alcohol Addiction Helpline is a free, 24 hours a day, 7 days a week helpline. It's never too late to seek help, so take the first step, for you and your loved ones.
Call 1-866-925-4030
     www.alcoholhotline.com

Ambiente Joven
(Website in Spanish) Ambiente Joven is dedicated to assisting LGBTQ Hispanic youth with their sexual and emotional health.
     www.ambientejoven.org

Gala Choruses
GALA Choruses, the Gay and Lesbian Association of Choruses, leads the North American LGBT choral movement with more than 170 member choruses and their 8,000 singers. They assist emerging choruses and facilitate networking and training for established groups. Currently, GALA Choruses is putting special focus on the implementation of programming that will assess and improve the sustainability of member choruses.

www.galachoruses.org

Gay, Lesbian, Bisexual and Transgender National Hotline
The Gay, Lesbian, Bisexual and Transgender National Hotline provides telephone and email peer-counseling, as well as factual information and local resources for cities and towns across the United States. The services are free and confidential. They can be reached at 1-888-843-4564

www.glnh.org/hotline

Gay, Lesbian and Straight Education Network: GLSEN
GLSEN works to ensure every student in every school, is valued and treated with respect, regardless of their sexual orientation, gender identity or gender expression. All students deserve a safe and affirming school environment where they can learn and grow.

www.glsen.org

Human Rights Campaign (HRC)
Human Rights Campaign represents more than 1.5 million members and supporters nationwide as the largest civil rights organization working to achieve equality for lesbian, gay, bisexual and transgender Americans.

www.hrc.org

It Gets Better
The It Gets Better Project's mission is to communicate to LGBTQ youth that the world around them gets better, and to create and inspire the changes needed to make it better for them.

www.itgetsbetter.org

Lambda Legal
Lambda Legal is the oldest and largest national legal organization whose mission is to achieve full recognition of the civil rights of lesbians, gay men, bisexuals, transgender people and those with HIV through impact litigation, education and public policy work.

www.lambdalegal.org

LGBT Friendly Campus Pride Index
The Campus Pride Index is a tool for assisting campuses in learning ways to improve their LGBT campus life and ultimately shape the educational experience to be more inclusive, welcoming and respectful of LGBT and Ally people.

www.campusprideindex.org

Maine Queer Youth Collaborative (MEQYC)
A collaborative effort to connect all Queer Youth resources in Maine.

www.facebook.com/MEQYC

Maine Trans Net
Maine Transgender Network, Inc. is a nonprofit organization that provides support and resources for the transgender community, families, and significant others, and raises awareness about the varied forms of gender identity and expression by providing training and consultation for mental health and social service professionals.

www.mainetransnet.org

The National Domestic Violence Hotline
The National Domestic Violence Hotline provides highly trained expert advocates are available 24/7 to talk confidentially with anyone experiencing domestic violence, seeking resources or questioning unhealthy aspects of their relationship. Contact them at

1-800-799-7233, 1-800-787-3224 (TTY)
www.thehotline.org

The National Runaway Safeline (NRS)
The NRS provides education and solution-focused interventions, offers non-sectarian, non-judgmental support, respects confidentiality, collaborates with volunteers, and responds to at-risk youth and their families 24 hours a day at, 1-800-786-2929.

www.1800runaway.org

New York City Anti-Violence Project (AVP)
AVP provides free and confidential assistance to thousands of lesbian, gay, bisexual, transgender, queer, and HIV-affected (LGBTQH) people each year from all five boroughs of New York City through direct client services, community organizing and public advocacy.

www.avp.org/index.php

The Not All Like That Christians Project: NALT
Christian churches, denominations and organizations have been working toward LGBTQ equality since 1964. The welcoming church movement currently includes some 5,000 congregations and about one million members.

notalllikethat.org

People with a Lesbian Gay Bisexual Transgender or Queer Parent: COLAGE
COLAGE unites people with lesbian, gay, bisexual, transgender, and/or queer parents into a network of peers and supports them as they nurture and empower each other.

www.colage.org

Trans Student Equality Resources (TSER)
TSER is a youth-led organization dedicated to improving the educational environment for trans (inclusive of all forms of gender non-conformity) and gender nonconforming students, affirming that one's gender identity is a valuable form of human diversity. The website offers a wide range of resources, including a list of conferences and camps for LGBTQ youth and adults.

www.transstudent.org

Trans Youth Equality Foundation
The Trans Youth Equality Foundation provides education, advocacy and support for transgender and gender non-conforming children and youth and their families.

www.transyouthequality.org

The Trevor Project
The Trevor Project is the leading national organization providing crisis intervention and suicide prevention services to LGBTQ young people ages 13-24. It is home to the only national 24/7 crisis intervention and suicide prevention lifeline for LGBTQ young people at:

1-866-488-7386

www.thetrevorproject.org/

Books

Faith matters: teenagers, sexuality, and religion.
Clapp, S., Helbert, K.L., & Zizak, A. (2003).
Fort Wayne, IN.: LifeQuest
Faith Matters presents the results of a national study of 5,819 teens from thirty different denominations showing how their faith and congregational activity related to their sexual values and behaviors.

God vs. Gay? The religious case for equality
Michaelson, J. (2011). Boston: Beacon Press.
Michaelson presents the argument that sexual diversity is part of nature and same sex families strengthen, not threaten, the religious values that people hold close. A thorough index of religious resources is provided.

Silent and undecided friends: motivating greater LGBT rights advocacy among clergy and congregations
Clapp, S. (2007). Christian Community, Inc.: LifeQuest
This report is based on surveys of 1,511 clergy from 32 different denominations: telephone interviews, with 268 clergy; among focus group meetings; and work with 61 pilot congregations. It looks at the attitudes of clergy toward LGBT people; the work of advocacy groups within denominations; and the issues that block full acceptance of LGBT people in congregations. The book provides a helpful resource section of LGBT and religious concerns.

Taking a new look: why congregations need LGBT members
Christian Community, Inc. (2008). Christian Community, Inc.: LifeQuest
This book highlights what a congregation may lose by not being welcoming and affirming of LGBT individuals. Reinforced by data from the Faith Matters Study, the book shows that the acceptance of LGBT people within congregations contributes to a positive image of Christianity and ultimately leads to growth within the church. Being welcoming and affirming also provides the church with an opportunity to offer sexuality education for youth, something which according to the statistics from Faith Matters is a much needed resource. Includes a good list of the available resources from Christian Community, short definitions section, and brief overview of some of the scripture related to homosexuality.

1640 Rhode Island Ave., NW
Washington, D.C. 20036
web: www.hrc.org
phone: 202-628-4160
fax: 202-347-5323

HUMAN
RIGHTS
CAMPAIGN®

ADDITIONAL ADVOCACY

Justice does not occur in a vacuum – it requires prophetic voices like yours engaging in community and public advocacy

Establishing and sustaining relationships with your elected officials is key to influencing their opinions on LGBT equality and the role of faith in public policy. Although meeting one-on-one with senators and representatives is, of course, the most direct way to communicate with them, there are many other ways to let your voice be heard. Here are a few ideas to enhance your community-based legislative advocacy:

- **Write an op-ed for your local paper.** For example: How does employment non-discrimination honor all workers in your community? How do your religious beliefs inform your position on legislation? Share your own journey about how you came to support/oppose a legislation-specific bill and, when fitting, include personal stories from family, friends, congregants, etc.

- **Write letters to the editor** in response to negative or offensive press regarding LGBT issues. Or, conversely, write a letter in support of a particularly powerful story. When writing letters, always keep your tone respectful. Sometimes journalists simply do not realize when their terms or situational structures are marginalizing and offensive to others, so assume best intentions when correcting them.

- **Attend a local town hall for your member of Congress** and ask questions about what they are doing in Washington to advance pro-LGBT policies. Be sure to identify yourself as a clergy person or a person of faith (remember, issue-based advocacy is fine for religious organizations to engage in).

- **Write an article for your congregation's newsletter** to educate congregants on the need for a fully inclusive ENDA or another LGBT-related issue, and encourage them to become politically active.

- **Host a letter-writing coffee hour** during Sunday School, adult religious education, or after your congregational services. Use this time to collect personal notes to elected officials requesting action on a piece of legislation. Consider making this a monthly event. Allow ample time for handwritten letters to arrive in Washington, or consider sending letters to the district office.

- **Designate a weekday for your congregation to make phone calls and e-mail members of Congress.** Organize a "coffee call" action day where congregants are encouraged to use part of their workday lunch or coffee break to make one phone call or send one e-mail to each elected official on an important piece of equality legislation. *Make sure to have plenty of reminders before the day of action.*

- **Designate a section of the congregation's main bulletin board for awareness about the Employment Non-Discrimination Act or other LGBT inclusion matters.**

- **Preach frequently about LGBT people, the issues they face and the hope for achieving full equality**

Being LGBT in the 21st Century

Liberty Hill
Foundation

Change. Not Charity.

Despite decades of proactive movements in support of the LGBT community, statistics indicate the road to justice and equality is still a long and daunting one. Suicide attempts are still high, and harassment at school is rampant.

Thought About Suicide

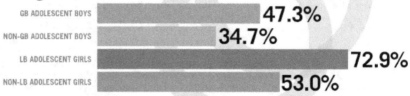

GB ADOLESCENT BOYS	47.3%
NON-GB ADOLESCENT BOYS	34.7%
LB ADOLESCENT GIRLS	72.9%
NON-LB ADOLESCENT GIRLS	53.0%

Attempted Suicide

GB ADOLESCENT BOYS	29.0%
NON-GB ADOLESCENT BOYS	12.6%
LB ADOLESCENT GIRLS	52.4%
NON-LB ADOLESCENT GIRLS	24.8%

Journal of Adolescent Health, 2006
(http://www.sprc.org/sites/sprc.org/files/library/SPRC_LGBT_Youth.pdf)

To make things worse, young adults in the LGBT community who lack parental support are significantly more at risk for depression and substance abuse.

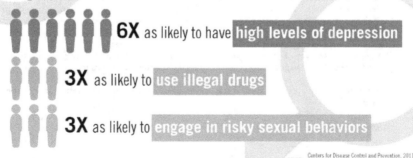

6X as likely to have **high levels of depression**

3X as likely to **use illegal drugs**

3X as likely to **engage in risky sexual behaviors**

Centers for Disease Control and Prevention, 2011

Another survey conducted with transgender students found they're more likely to come out to their peers than to school staff...

66%
to Peers

44%
to School Staff

...Although their peers are more likely to do damage. More than half of transgender students reported physical **harassment at school**, and almost all of them reported verbal abuse from peers.

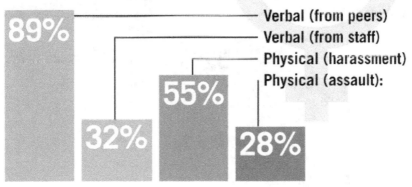

89%

55%

32%

28%

Verbal (from peers)
Verbal (from staff)
Physical (harassment)
Physical (assault):

Gay, Lesbian and Straight Education Network, 2009
(http://www.glsen.org/cgi-bin/iowa/all/library/record/2388.html?state=research&type=research)

But There's Hope for the Future

Columbia University researcher Mark Hatzenbuehler determined five key elements that improve the quality of a LGBT teen's life at school. They are:

Anti-bullying policies

Gay-Straight Alliances

Anti-discrimination policies

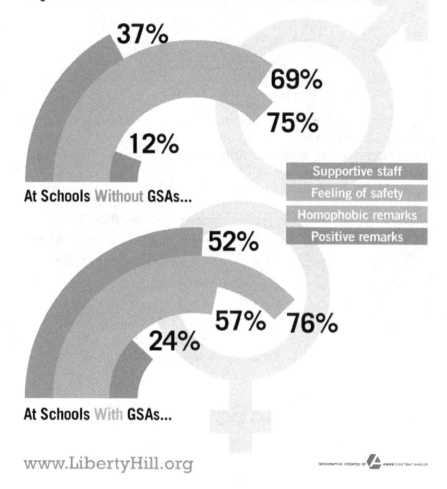

Higher proportion of same-sex couples

Higher proportion of Democrats in the county

Pediatrics, 2011
(http://www.healthnews.com/en/news/Social-environment-linked-to-gay-teen-suicide-risk/18_ZI$vMD34euQihd9MXG$/)

...And he's right. LGBT students at schools with support groups such as a Gay-Straight Alliance report a more positive experience than LGBT students without similar outlets..

37%

69%

75%

12%

At Schools Without **GSAs...**

Supportive staff

Feeling of safety

Homophobic remarks

Positive remarks

52%

57% 76%

24%

At Schools With **GSAs...**

www.LibertyHill.org

INFOGRAPHIC CREATED BY AMOS CONTENT GROUP

Liberty Hill is a non-profit organization based in Los Angeles working to advance social change through a strategic combination of grants, leadership training, and campaigns. This infographic is to help people realize what is at stake for lesbian, gay, bisexual and transgender youth.

Glossary of LGBTQ-Related Terms

The glossary is designed to provide basic definitions of words and phrases commonly used in discussions sex, gender, and sexuality related issues. All language is constantly evolving; new terms are introduced, while others fade from use or change in meaning over time. The same word may mean different things to different people. It is always a good idea to respect the manner in which someone choses to self identify and the language that person prefers.

This glossary was compiled from the Gay, Lesbian, and Straight Education Network's (GLSEN) Safe Space Kit; The Wateville Inclusive Community Project's Stand Up Action Toolkit; The GLAAD Media Reference Guide; the Rainbow Project; and the UC Berkeley Gender Equity Resource Center.

Ally: A member of the majority or dominant group who works to end oppression by supporting or advocating for the oppressed population. For example, any non-LGBTQ person who supports and stands up for the equality of LGBTQ people, sometimes referred to as a "straight ally," or, an adult who supports LGBTQ youth.

Androgynous: Having the characteristics or nature of both masculinity and femininity.

Asexual: A person who does not feel sexual attraction to anyone.

Biphobia: Fear of or aversion to bisexuality or bisexual people.

Bisexual: A sexual orientation and/or identity of a person who is sexually and emotionally attracted to some males and some females.

Cisgender: Refers to people whose gender identity and expression are aligned with their sex assigned at birth.

Coming Out: Declaring one's identity, specifically, being lesbian, gay, bisexual or transgender, whether to a person in private or a group of people. To be "in the closet" means to hide one's identity.

Drag: The theatrical performance of one or more genders, often involving the presentation of exaggerated, stereotypical gender characteristics.

Dyke: Derogatory term for a lesbian. Origin uncertain. Literally a dam or a bank, it could be a sexual reference to blocking a passage. Or it could come from "buildyker" a dam-builder, referring to a macho stereotype. Some lesbians have reclaimed the term and use it as an affirmation.

Equality: The concept that all people should be treated as equals and be given the same political, economic, social, and civil rights.

Equal Opportunities: The concept that everyone should have equal access to jobs, services, housing, medical care etc. whatever their race, ability, age, sexual orientation, gender, etc.

Faggot; Fag: A derogatory term for a gay or bisexual man (or sometimes any queer person). Literally a bundle of sticks that fuel a fire. Thought to relate to a medieval tradition of throwing 'sodomites' onto the fire whilst burning convicted criminals at the stake as a form of execution.

Family of Choice: Persons or group of people an individual sees as significant in their life. It may include none, all, or some members of their family of origin. In addition, it may include individuals such as significant others, domestic partners, friends, and coworkers.

FTM or F2M (female-to-male): An identity of a person who was assigned female at birth, and who identifies as male.

Gay: A sexual orientation and/or identity of a person who is sexually and emotionally attracted to some members of the same sex. Although gay can refer to both males and females, many prefer the term "lesbian" for females. Gay is sometimes used as an umbrella term to refer to all lesbian, gay and bisexual people, but some prefer the more inclusive term "LGBTQ" or "queer."

Gender: A social construct based on a group of emotional, behavioral, and cultural characteristics often referred to as feminine, masculine, androgynous, or other. Gender can be understood to have several components, including gender identity, gender expression, and gender role.

Gender Binary: The concept there are two genders: man and woman and a person must identify as either/or.

Gender Expression: The manner in which people express their gender identity through appearance, dress, mannerisms, speech patterns, and social interactions.

Gender Identity: How we identify ourselves in terms of our gender. Identities may be: male, female, androgynous, transgender and others.

Gender-Neutral Pronoun: A pronoun that does not associate a gender with the person being discussed. Two of the most common gender-neutral pronouns are "zie" (xe, ze) replacing she and he, and "hir" (xem, zir) replacing her and him. Some people choose to use "they" and "them" as singular pronouns to avoid gender identification.

Gender Non-Conforming or Gender Variant: An identity of a person who does not conform to traditional or societal binary gender expectations.

Gender Orientation: Individuals internal sense of their gender. Gender orientation doesn't necessarily align with the sex assigned at birth.

Gender Role: The social expectations of how an individual should act, think and/or feel based upon one's assigned biological sex. A set of traditional and stereotypical roles, traits, dress, characteristics, qualities, mannerisms and behaviors that are associated with societal norms of masculine men and feminine females.

Genderism: The systematic belief that there are only two genders: men and women and that masculinity is attached to male bodies and femininity is attached to female bodies.

Genderqueer: An identity of people who identify as and/or express themselves as somewhere in the continuum between masculinity and femininity or outside of the gender binary system. Gender-queer people may or may not identify as LGBT.

Heterosexism: Applies to attitudes, bias, and discrimination in favor of heterosexuality and relationships. It includes the presumption that everyone is heterosexual or that male/female attractions and relationships are the norm and therefore superior. It is the belief that everyone is or should be straight.

Heterosexual: A sexual orientation and/or identity of a person who is sexually and emotionally attracted to some members of another sex (specifically, a male who is attracted to some females or a female who is attracted to some males). Often referred to as "straight."

Homophobia: Fear of or aversion to homosexuality or lesbian, gay or bisexual people.

Homosexual: An identity of people who are sexually and emotion-ally attracted to some members of their own sex; originated in the medical and psychological professions. Currently, many prefer the term lesbian or gay.

Institutional Oppression: Arrangement of a society used to benefit one group at the expense of another through the use of language, media education, religion, economics, etc.

Internalized Oppression: The process by which an oppressed person comes to believe, accept, or live out the inaccurate stereotypes and misinformation about their group.

Intersex: A general term used for a person born with reproductive or sexual anatomy that doesn't seem to fit the typical definitions of female or male. Intersex variances can affect the genitals, the chro-mosomes, and/or secondary sex characteristics.

Lambda: The Gay Activist Alliance originally chose the lambda, the Greek letter "L", as a symbol in 1970. Organizers chose the letter "L" to signify liberation. The word has become a way of expressing the concept "lesbian and gay male" in a minimum of syllables and has been adopted by such organizations as Lambda Legal Defense and Education Fund.

Lesbian: A sexual orientation and/or identity of a person who is female-identified and who is sexually and emotionally attracted to some other females.

LGBTQ: An umbrella term referring collectively to people who identify as lesbian, gay, bisexual and/or transgender, those who identify as questioning and/or queer, intersex, asexual, and more. The "+" is a symbol of inclusivity for those who do not identify as L,G,B,T,Q,I, or A. In the past "gay" was used as a general, overarching term, but currently the more inclusive terms LGBT, LGBTQ, and LGBTQIA+ are regularly used and preferred by many LGBTQ people and allies. The word "queer" is also frequently used as an umbrella term to include a wide range of sex, genders, and sexuality combinations.

MTF or M2F (male-to-female): An identity of a person who was assigned male at birth, and who identifies as female.

Non-Op: A trans-identified person whose identity does not involve receiving Sexual Reassignment Surgery/Sex Confirmation Surgery.

On T: When a person takes the hormone testosterone.

Pansexual: A sexual orientation and/or identity of a person who is sexually and emotionally attracted to people regardless of their gender expression and/or identity.

Post-Op: A trans-identified person who has received Sexual Reassignment Surgery/Sex Confirmation Surgery.

Pre-Op: A trans-identified person who has not received Sexual Reassignment Surgery; implies that the person does intend to receive such surgical procedures.

Pride: An affirmation of one's self and the LGBTQ community as a whole. The modern 'pride' movement began after the Stonewall riots in 1969. Pride marches are common in western societies.

Queer: An umbrella term used to describe a sexual orientation, gender identity, or gender expression that does not conform to heteronormative society. While it is used as a neutral, or even a positive term among many LGBTQ people today, historically it has been used negatively and is still considered derogatory by many.

Questioning: An identity of people who are uncertain of their sexual orientation and/or identity and/or their gender identity.

Sex or Biological Sex: This can be considered our "packaging" and is determined by our chromosomes (often XX or XY), our hormones, and our internal and external genitalia. Typically, we are assigned the sex of male or female at birth, though some are born intersex.

Sex Reassignment Surgery (SRS)/Sex Confirmation Surgery: A term used by some medical professionals to refer to a group of surgical options that alter a person's sex to match their sex identity.

Sexual Behavior: What we do sexually and with whom.

Sexual Identity: What we call ourselves in terms of our sexuality. Such labels include "lesbian," "gay," "bisexual," "queer," "heterosexual," "straight," among many more.

Sexual Orientation: A person's emotional and/or sexual attraction toward others.

Sodomy; Sodomy laws: Anal or oral copulation with a member of the same or opposite sex. Derived from the story of Sodom and Gommorah, in the book of Genesis. Historically used to selectively persecute gay people. These were ruled unconstitutional by the U.S Supreme Court in Lawrence v. Texas (2003).

Stereotype: A set of overly simplistic generalizations about a group of people that allows others to categorize them and treat them accordingly.

Transgender: An identity of people whose gender identity is not aligned with their sex assigned at birth and/or whose gender expression is non-conforming.

Transition: The variety of actions a person may take to transition from one gender/sex identity to another. These may include social, psychological and/or medical processes. Transitioning is a complex process that occurs over a long period of time, not a one-time event.

Transphobia: Fear of or aversion to transgender people or those who are perceived to break or blur societal norms regarding gender identity or gender expression.

Transsexual: A term, originated in medical and psychological communities, that historically referred to people whose gender identity was not aligned with their sex assigned at birth.

Triangle: A symbol of remembrance. Gay men in the Nazi concentration camps were forced to wear the pink triangle as a designation of being homosexual. Women who did not conform to social roles, often believed to be lesbians, had to wear the black triangle. The triangles are worn today as symbols of freedom, reminding us to never forget.

Two-Spirit (also Two Spirit or Twospirit): Used in many Native American communities to refer to people who are lesbian, gay, bisexual, transgender or gender non-conforming. The term usually implies a masculine spirit and a feminine spirit living in the same body and has been adopted by some contemporary lesbian, gay, bisexual and transgender Native Americans to describe themselves.

Ze: Gender neutral pronouns that can be used instead of he/she.

Zir: Gender neutral pronouns that can be used instead of his/her.

Awards and Achievements, O&A Vol. 1

Portlander Doing More With Less (Start-up Youth Program)
The League of Young Voters 2009

Maine Literary Award for Best Anthology
Maine Writers and Publishers Alliance 2012

What We're Reading
Teaching Tolerance, a program of the Southern Poverty Law Center
"Out and Allied: An Anthology of Performance Pieces gives center stage to a compelling collection of plays, poems and monologues written by LGBTQ youth and their allies. The chapters on presentation, production, writing and leadership transform this anthology into a young activist's handbook."
www.tolerance.org/magazine/number-42-fall-2012/department/what-we-re-reading

Editor Bios

Cathy Plourde is the founder and director of Add Verb, and has presented on theatre and social change, health and wellness nationally and internationally. Her plays The Thin Line and You the Man have traveled the US and Australia.

Meghan Brodie is an Assistant Professor of Theatre and a faculty member in the Women and Gender Studies program at the University of Southern Maine. She teaches dramatic literature, theatre history, text analysis, and acting and also works as a director, playwright, and dramaturg. Meghan holds a Ph.D. from Cornell University.

Elisa Orme, LMSW, recently graduated from UNE, feels strongly about the inadequacies and failings of the criminal justice system and hopes to contribute to positive changes. She wants to explore unconventional places social work can be practiced.

Jack Whelan graduated University College Dublin in 2012 with a Masters in History. He currently works for Add Verb as an editor and social media intern. In his spare time, he publishes ebooks and moderates an online gay men's interest community.

Zabet NeuCollins is currently an undergraduate at the College of the Atlantic in Bar Harbor, ME. She is studying human ecology, which to her is a mélange of anthropology, applied arts, and environmental concern. She is set to emerge in the real world in 2015.

Performance Pieces by Theme
Many of these pieces are readily adaptible to reflect different sexual orientations, biological sex, gender identity or gender expression. Please feel free to make changes that also honor the intentions of the writers.

Homophobia

Humorous

Judgment

Love

Trans

*these pieces are not neccessarily trans-specific, but are readily adaptible to reflect different sexual orientations, biological sex, gender identity or gender expression.

Trust

CPSIA information can be obtained
at www.ICGtesting.com
Printed in the USA
FSHW012057281218
54708FS